Amazon Warriors:

An Introduction

A. P. Bristol

Strategic Book Publishing
New York, New York

Strategic Book Publishing
An imprint of Writers Literary & Publishing
    Services, Inc.
845 Third Avenue, 6th Floor – 6016
New York, NY 10022
http://www.strategicbookpublishing.com

ISBN: 978-1-60860-060-1
SKU: 1-60860-060-2

Printed in the United States of America

Book Design: Judy Maenle

*This book is dedicated to my long-suffering wife
for her forbearance and to my family
for their love and support.*

Acknowledgements

First of all I would like to thank Dr. Jeannine Davis-Kimball for sparing time from her busy schedule to answer my questions;

Dr. Farid Alakbarli for his permission to use his material;

My agents, for their encouragement and my publisher for their courage in taking me aboard;

Last, but not least, the Open University and my tutors for their unstinting help over the years. Without their help and support this book would never have been written.

Contents

Abbreviations Used

AS	Museum Antikensammlungen, Munich
BM	British Museum
IN Ref xx	Internet Reference number xx
Kimball	Dr. Jeannine Davis-Kimball, 2002
Kleinbaum	Wettan-Kleinbaum, Abby, 1983
OCCC	Oxford Companion to Classical Civilisation, 1998
RFV	Red Figure Vases, Archaic Period. John Boardman, 1975
Wilde	Lyn Webster-Wilde, 1999

Preface

The problem of the Amazon Warriors of Classical Greece is something of a knotty one, and so I have not attempted to make any sort of decision as to whether or not they really existed, although many people are convinced that they did. What I have attempted to do is simply to provide a very brief introduction to the problem, the answer to which no one agrees about. I have also attempted to provide avenues for further research for those who would like to travel that road. The bibliography contains some excellent references to scholarly works and these are well worth a follow-up. Do not be put off by the scholarly tag; it is really only to indicate the level of expertise involved, and they are all eminently readable and enjoyable. So far as the Internet references go, one will need to make an informed decision as to whether or not they should be pursued. Unfortunately, there are many web sites on the Internet that only pay lip-service to the Classical Amazons, dealing as they do with female body-building and women's clubs with an Amazon name tag. Even among the more genuine sites, care must be taken not to take anything at face value unless it is properly referenced, so that one can follow it up and confirm the accuracy of the information presented. There was more than one type of Amazon Warrior, for example, Thermodontine and Libyan, of which more are in the text. I have mentioned more than one different theory as to their origins, but I must leave it to the reader to reach an informed decision by completing his or her own research as to which theory, if any, does in fact hold up under close scrutiny. There are also many legends and illustrations, especially on vases and of course the sculptures on the pediment of the Acropolis, which make it seem as though they must have existed, but much of the information has been passed down by word of mouth with all the inaccuracy that entails. However, although Herodotus of Halicarnassus lived long after the Trojan War, c. 490/480–429/425 BC, a considerable amount that he wrote about has, in fact, been proven to be quite accurate. Witness, for example, the finding of Troy (also known as Ilion) by Heinrich Schliemann. He took Herodotus at his word, followed the geography in his writings, and in doing so found the site where so much action took place during that war. At least, to qualify that slightly, Schliemann found the site of several Troys built upon each other and only failed to identify the exact level upon which Priam's Troy was built. "Schliemann discovered the first five settlements and identified Troy II with the Homeric Troy. Dorpfeld's discoveries, confirmed by Blegen, proved that the Homeric Troy must be identified with Troy VIIA, which was destroyed by fire about the accepted date of the Trojan War. The tradition is believed to reflect a real war between the Greeks of the late Mycenaean period and the inhabitants of the Troad, or Troas, in Anatolia, part of present day Turkey. Modern archaeological excavations have shown that Troy was destroyed by fire in the early twelfth century BC, the traditional date of the war, and that the war may actually have resulted from the desire either to plunder the wealthy city or to put an end to Troy's commercial control of the Dardanelles." (www.mnsu.edu/emuseum/archaeology/sites/europe/ hissarlik.html)

Somewhat unfortunately the find took place before modern values and ways of excavation and conservation had been properly explored and laid down. Because Schliemann more or less bull-dozed his way right through the centre of the mound at Hissarlik ("Place of Fortresses"), much valuable information has been lost to our modern archaeologists and to posterity. To be fair to Schliemann, he did not have the advantages that modern science has provided for our use, and we must recognise that he did sterling work in finding the cities of Troy. The region around Hissarlik is still inhabited by the descendants of the many and varied peoples who laid claim to the ancient land of Anatolia. Present day Canakkale is a thriving small town close to the ancient site, which lies on both sides of the Dardanelles and touches both Europe (Gelibolu Peninsula) and Asia (Biga Peninsula). Just as it was in the time immortalised by Homer, maritime traffic connects both sides of the straits. Today passenger ferries travel the waters close to where the warring tribes of Greeks and Trojans once fought a battle that went down in history and is still talked about.

Aside from the Middle East, as peoples migrated westward, it is a possibility that some Scythians went along with them. When we look at the westward migration of the Celts from Middle Europe around 300 BC as far as Wales and Ireland, it seems as though this could be the case. There are stories of warrior queens, both in Ireland and Wales, who fit the bill as Amazon warriors or Eurasian nomads. Comparisons have been made and similarities noted between the art forms of animals in Celtic art and the animal style of the Eurasian nomads. Obviously the resemblances noted are assumed to have travelled westward with the influx of nomads. There are many examples of strong Irish women mentioned in the Mythology Cycle, a strong warrior queen being Medb of Connacht. She was a sensuous, intelligent woman who incited Cú Chulainn to defend Ulster against the thievery and depredations of her army, led by an Ulster warrior named Fergus whom she had seduced into co-operation. Cú Chulainn won battle after battle until Ulster emerged victorious. As something of an aside at this point, most people assume that the name Tara is Irish, as in Tara's Halls, the Harp of Tara, etc. Not so. It apparently arrived with the influx of the middle European peoples or Celts and was eventually adopted by the Irish.

However, enough of this preamble. We will try to identify and place the Classical Amazons about whom so much has been written and believed even to the present day. I trust that I will inspire at least one reader to continue along this road and perhaps even encourage a life-long interest in the study of Classical times.

Chapter 1

Introduction

The ancient Greeks lived their lives surrounded by divine, semi-divine, and mythological beings, some of whom will be familiar to everyone. Examples of them would be Zeus (Roman Jupiter), Athena (Minerva), and Artemis (Diana), not forgetting Herakles and Theseus. There are many others, but I think these should suffice to illustrate my meaning. Amongst our legacy of writings from Ancient Greek writers and playwrights such as Homer, Herodotus, Thucydides, Euripides, Aristophanes, and Strabo, to name but a few, there are many stories about a race of female warriors called Amazons (Αμαζονες). Tales and legends of them cling to the area around the Black Sea, or the Euxine Sea (Sweet Waters, as it was known in the past), and to the Caucasus region. They were also apparently to be found in Libya and India, but we have to consider the question—were there ever any Amazon warriors in antiquity? This is not an easy question to answer, because there is quite likely to be an equal number of theories as to their existence or non-existence as there are scholars. References to the Amazons in Ancient Greek literature, paintings, and sculpture are many and varied, and attempting to separate the wheat from the chaff can be quite a difficult proposition. The problem is exacerbated by the ancient authors being unable to fully agree with each other, even though they were so much closer in time to the Amazons. Modern authors are not in much more agreement with each other for that matter.

Research into the Classical Amazons is more than a little limited when compared with, say, the Ancient Greek theatre and quite often contradictory, but the intrigue of a dominant race of warrior women from the Greek Bronze Age, possibly even descended from or linked in some fashion with the Minoan civilisation of Crete of the third to second millennium BC has flourished from ancient times right up to the present day. The ancient Greeks undoubtedly believed in the Amazons and their exploits and wove many stories around them. Many people today have heard of some of the more famous Amazons: women like Andromache, whose name means Man Fighter; Andromeda (Ruler of Men); Hippolyte (Of the Stampeding Horse); Melanippe (Black Mare); and probably one of the most famous of all, Penthesilea (Compelling Men to Mourn). Queen Penthesilea, of course, was one of the Amazon heroines at the Battle for Troy, and we are also told that Melanippe was actually one of the Amazons who was shipwrecked on the Scythian coast and one of those who met up with the Scythian men mentioned by Herodotus.

Many of the Amazons' names have something to do with either fighting or horses, and there are, of course, many more than I have mentioned. Some listings of their names and meanings may be found on various web sites such as the one just mentioned, the address of which is to be found in the bibliography. With regard to the names of the Amazons, the confusion factor can be quite high at times since there appears to be several warriors who use the same name, sometimes at the same time. We must therefore be careful to try to identify the warrior we are talking or writing about. An example who comes to mind is Hippolyte, of whom there were at least two at a similar point in time. One of these was a queen who owned the belt that Herakles was sent to retrieve, and the other was the sister of Penthesilea. This was the one who was killed in a hunting accident by Penthesilea after which, in her shame, Penthesilea went off to Troy in order to be purified by King Priam and to atone for the death.

However, at this point in time no one has provided empirical proof of the existence of the Amazon warriors, and despite many excavations in the lands where the Amazons were supposed to frequent, no "Amazon" graves have been discovered. That, of course, could be because no one knows what to expect to see in an Amazon grave, but graves of women warriors have been found and documented as we shall see later. In his discussion of the Heroic Age, Burckhardt says that his view is that the Greeks invented the Amazon character (Burckhardt, 1998, 154). And W. B. Tyrrell's thought is that the evidence from Athens does not prove that Amazons existed, but simply that the myth did. For Tyrrell, the mythopoeia of the Amazons was done by men in "pursuit of their own aims and goals." However, Lysias does not appear to agree with either of these gentlemen and says, "In ancient times were the Amazons, daughters of Ares, dwelling beside the river Thermodon; they alone of the people round were armed with iron, and they first of all to mount horses." (Lamb, 1930, 2.4). We must remember, of course, that Lysias lived some two and a half millennia before these modern scholars, but it does help to indicate some of the conflict between various authorities about the Amazons. Can we find out one way or another who, if anyone, is right?

Fighting ability in ancient societies was usually the yardstick by which social status was determined. The style of the Greek hoplites and Roman warriors favoured men in battle because of the fact that they had the necessary upper body strength, but the fighting style which was attributed to the Amazons and others such as the Scythians and Hittites favoured the women much more. Mounted archers, lithe and agile, could compete very favourably with the men because of the speed of attack and retreat and the fact that hand-to-hand combat was not necessarily a requirement of battle. The speed of the attack and retreat and the famous Parthian "parting shot," in which they were able to shoot arrows over the horses tail at the enemy whilst galloping on the retreat, made them very effective killers, equal to the men. This gave them a much higher status than they would otherwise have had if they had simply been wives and mothers. Horses, bows and arrows empowered these warrior women to be a serious threat when met in opposition on the battlefield.

The earliest references to the Amazons, rather than simply women warriors, was of their participation in the siege of Troy in approximately 1185 BC, but this was not recorded until Homer composed his famous *Iliad* some four hundred years after the event. Although Homer was not specific about who was actually involved in the siege of Troy, other writers say that the Amazon Queen Penthesilea and her warriors came to the aid of King Priam and that she displayed great bravery in battle, killing many Greek soldiers. Her end came when she was killed in battle by the Greek hero Achilles, who after he had killed her and removed her helmet, was overcome with emotion at the sight of her beauty—much too late of course. There are references to other Amazons of note as well, such as Andromache and Hippolyte.

Many stories are told about Theseus, King of Athens, including his slaying of the Minotaur before he became King; he was also well known as an abductor of women. The Minotaur was the offspring of Pasiphae, the wife of Minos, and a bull for which she developed a passion. King Minos of Crete habitually sacrificed an unblemished bull to Poseidon annually, except that one year he did not, because he desired it himself. Poseidon took grave exception to this lack of respect and so instigated this passion of Pasiphae. She had Daedalus construct a mêchanêma in the form of a cow, and Pasiphae climbed inside it so that she could mate with the bull. The Minotaur was the horrific result, a human infant born with the head and horns of a bull and a tail. Daedalus was then commissioned to construct the Labyrinth in which the Minotaur was imprisoned.

War between Athens and Minos had come about because Andregeos, son of Minos, was assassinated at the Panathenaic festival on the orders of Aegeus, father of Theseus, who had Andregeos killed because he won every prize during the feast. To compound the error of war a drought ensued; to combat which the Athenians asked for the help of Apollo, who told them that only when they had appeased Minos for the death of his son would the drought be ended. As tribute to King Minos, therefore, Athens had to provide seven youths and seven maidens on a regular basis for sacrifice to the monster. Theseus, however, with the aid of Ariadne, daughter of Minos, defeated the monster in single combat and effectively put paid to the tribute of youths and maidens from Athens (Figure 1).

Figure 1. Theseus killing the Minotaur, from the tondo of a cup by Apollodorus.

The problem with fighting the Minotaur was that it lived in the Labyrinth, and once inside the maze the adventurer was unable to find his way out again, so cunningly was it laid out. Ariadne, bright girl, provided Theseus with a ball of string so that he could attach it to the entrance and pay it out as he penetrated the maze. All he then had to do was to slay the beast and follow the string back to the entrance again. Such a simple solution to the problem. Strange that our hero Theseus had to depend on a woman to think of it. Perhaps it was a situation of all brawn and no brains, although we have no way of knowing now.

Although Theseus was built up as a hero figure, other tales are told of his darker side such as his killing of his son, Hippolytus after being accused of rape by Phaedra, wife of Theseus. There are also stories of his abduction and rape of Amazon women, some of which link him with Herakles and his Labours. Theseus and Herakles were both Greek heroes and ostensibly distinguished themselves many times by defeating Amazons in hand-to-hand combat, because defeating Amazons was proof positive of their heroism and warrior's prowess. Conquering barbarians, as the Amazons, the Persians, and pretty well anyone else who was not Greek were classed, was an assertion of Athenian values and superior civilisation. All of the stories which centred around the Greeks versus Amazons, Greeks versus Persians, and Greeks versus anyone else end with the Greek soldiers winning the various battles, generally contriving to emerge on top, and being portrayed as heroic soldiers who were unbeatable in battle. Like individual Trojans, the Amazons were highly praised by the Greeks for their strength, courage, and endurance, but they inevitably lost their battles to the Greeks. As Blok would have it, the Amazons were similar to the Trojans in that they were valiant warriors as individuals, but they only existed in order to be defeated (Blok, 1994, 435).

These ways of thinking may perhaps be in agreement with Tyrrell, that the Amazon Warrior was simply a construct of the Greeks, thought up so that the Greeks would always have reason to think that they were invincible. This would help to encourage the common soldiers to think that they were indeed a force to be reckoned with, in order to reinforce the Greek perception of themselves. Even now, in modern times, Fiada thinks that the modern Greek has the highest insecurity factor in the world, and that his efforts go towards covering up his self-doubts (Fiada, 2000, 14), although I think we must treat such comments with a certain amount of caution. Another reason could be, of course, simply to do with keeping badly behaved women under control—in their place, if you like. It could be that this was the main reason, and any other benefit it brought was a bonus.

Jason, during his adventures with the Argonauts is credited (or discredited depending on your point of view) with saying, "We are in a sad way if our homeward journey depends on women." A revealing and rather thoughtless remark perhaps when we consider that he took all the help he could get from Medea, without whom he could never have obtained the Golden Fleece. One of the tasks which Jason [Iason] had to perform was to yoke a pair of fire breathing bulls and plough a field with them. Because Jason promised to take her home with him as his wife, Medea aided and abetted him by providing him with a magic fire retardant ointment so that he could not be burned. Obviously he succeeded in yoking the bulls, etc., and so Aietes, King of Kolchis, sent him off to where the fleece was guarded by a rather large and probably bad-tempered serpent. Again Medea stepped in and helped Jason to put the serpent to sleep, and so our hero sailed on his merry way homeward with the Golden Fleece and a new bride. Another heroic reputation was enhanced by female intelligence.

The Amazons were essentially anti-Greek and anti-establishment and as such were depicted as androgynous hard-riding, hard-fighting females, who could, in the main, exist without men. They rejected the ultimate Greek female experience of marriage and instead engaged in the men's world of war and fighting. This was completely opposite to the way of life of upper class Greek women. They stayed at home spinning, weaving, and looking after the oikos in which they ostensibly reigned supreme, but they were not allowed the sort of freedom that was enjoyed by the Amazons. I say "ostensibly" because the men carried the keys to the store-rooms, did the shopping, and ensured that their womenfolk were kept in seclusion. This type of situation was used to effect by Aristophanes in his comedy "Ekklesiazusae" in which the women dressed as men and took over the Assembly.

In fact, what we have here is a situation that was totally outside anything known to the male Athenians, who perhaps felt that their position as law-givers, protectors, and soldiers was undermined by the reputation of the Amazons, which subsequently made them appear less manly than they thought of themselves. Therefore something needed to be done to boost their own self-image, thus giving rise to the encounters between Greek and Amazon in which the Greeks inevitably came out on top. Myths and legends held a great power over the Greeks and were accepted as fact by them. So the tales of the Amazons told by the Greeks were, I think, supposed in part to be a salutary lesson to the Greek women as to what could happen if they went astray. The fact that they ignored the men, their lords and masters, and took their lives into their own hands would put the upper class Greek women on the slippery downward slope to poor reputations, promiscuity, and maybe even death, which was most definitely not the way they had been brought up. The point was made in every story that the men would always win in the end, and this raised the very obvious question of what was the point in the women causing themselves all the pain of disobedience and terror of warfare when they could not win anyway. Kentaurs and Amazons were the sort of barbarian that the Greek heroes had to conquer to prove their bravery and heroism. They were not seen as a negligible threat, and so to defeat them was obviously an assertion of a superior civilisation.

Keeping alive the stories and myths of old, many modern authors have written books specifically about the Amazons. Others have included short sections in their books about other subjects, for example vase painting, but short or not, it is still included. Sue Blundell (1999) wrote about "Women in Ancient Greece" and devoted a full chapter to the Amazons. Other modern authors whom we can consider are Josine Blok, "The Early Amazons: Modern and Ancient Perspectives on a Persistent Myth" (1995); William Blake Tyrrell, who wrote "Amazons: A Study in Athenian Mythmaking" (1984); Jeannine Kimball-Davis' "Women Warriors" (2002); and "Early Greek Myths" by Timothy Gantz (1993). For illustrations of the myths we can turn to several of Boardman's books, including his "Black Figure Vases" and his "Red Figure Vases," as well as Rasmussen and Spivey's "Looking at Greek Vases" (1997). Another interesting book is Smith's "Hellenistic Sculpture" (1991) in which we can see scenes of Amazonomachy from temple friezes.

Although there are many Amazon websites, of which a small number is included in the bibliography, the major website devoted to women and gender studies is Διοτιμα (Diotima), the full address of which is listed in the bibliography and contains much information about women and gender in ancient times. The Perseus Project web site has a considerable amount of information about Ancient Greece, and there are also several websites devoted to modern women who consider themselves to be Amazons and who try to emulate their heroes even to the extent of living by themselves without men. All of this helps to keep alive the myths and legends of the Amazon nation but without any proof of their existence being offered. These superficial types of websites appear to be simply women's clubs for the vociferous, giving them a cause to champion; they are for the easily impressionable, to give them something to dream about away from their daily lives and for those who aspire to the supposed physical appearance of the ancient warriors. Some of the web sites dedicated to female body-building are listed in the bibliography, for example, the American female body-building, but there is a feed on the site called "amaz0ns." (Yes, there is a zero in the name.) Unfortunately this only proved to be more of the same, apparently run by lesbians for lesbians. Other web sites, however, are much more knowledgeable. Common with most of them is that they have a major tendency to make statements without providing any references to back them up. Many of them appear to be the product of wishful thinking and are therefore quite subjective, to say the least.

As you can imagine, therefore, there is a distinct question mark over whether or not the Amazons actually existed in the real world. Modern digs in the Ukraine and Southern Russia suggest that they or at least tribes of women warriors did exist and the archaeology of the area has convinced Professor Renate Rolle and Dr. Jeannine Davis-Kimball of this fact. The oldest female warrior's grave so far excavated dates from the fourth century BC, but unfortunately this is much later than their earliest mention by the ancient authors, and so the search for earlier graves of women warriors continues. In the light of all of the archaeology so far unearthed, the home page of the Pygmalion Project agrees that there is no reason to deny any reality of ancient women warriors because of the supporting evidence, but the question that it does not answer still remains as to whether or not they were in fact the classical Amazons. So it would appear, therefore, that evidence is building a case in favour of tribes of women warriors and possibly some sort of Amazon warriors actually existing, but so far without, according to the Greeks, the several different tribes being distinguished from each other.

Another aspect already mentioned that should be taken into consideration is that of gender reversal. The whole Amazon story turns upon its head the total way of life of the upper class Greek men and women and in all probability left the men at least, with feelings of insecurity, which is probably why in all of the Greek/Amazon and Greek/kentaur encounters the Greeks win. The Greeks led a patrilineal, patriarchal, polarised way of life and found the matriarchal way difficult to understand or even to appreciate.

The playwrights, however, exploited this aspect in plays like Aeschylus' "The Agamemnon." In this Clytemnestra, wife of Agamemnon, was cast as a strong-minded independent woman with some qualities similar to the ancient Amazons and who took on the might of Agamemnon and won. For a short time only, however, until Orestes overcame the rebel and gained revenge for his father's murder. Again, we have the old story—the men defeat the women. Another playwright who used gender reversal was Aristophanes in his "Ekklesiazusae" and in his absolutely hilarious and rude "Thesmophoriazusae." In this he had Agathon the playwright dress as a woman for the sake of inspiration while writing his plays and Mnesilochus (a kinsman) cross-dress as a sort of antihero trying to save his nephew Euripides from a death sentence caused by his past actions concerning the women of Athens. It would seem that Euripides gave away many of the secrets of methods that were used by the women to run things in the background and that they did not want exposed to view. This decided them to declare a vendetta against Euripides, who promptly went very pale at the thought and attempted to have someone speak, nay, plead for him at the celebration. In the event, only Mnesilochus was daft enough to pit himself against the might of the women, and he failed miserably.

In his famous anti-war play "Lysistrata" she of the title role was cast as the leader of a consortium of women from Sparta, Boeotia, Megara, and Athens. The women took on some of the qualities that were to be expected from the Amazons, overcame the fighting men of each area, and essentially blackmailed them into putting an end to the war. Their attitude was "stop the war or there will be no sex" and although the play itself is very funny and quite rude in places, it really was a plea to stop fighting and settle down peacefully. The play ended very well, but alas, not so in real life.

What I would like to do is to look at the mythological background of the Amazons, with consideration of some modern interpretations of the legendary Amazon warriors and also to see if modern archaeology can perhaps lend some credence to the stories, by examining the evidence in the digs in the Ukraine and Southern Russia.

A considerable number of tombs have been excavated and documented by Jeannine Davis-Kimball, along with people like Professor Rolle and her associates in the Steppes. Other authors such as the journalist Webster-Wilde (1999) and perhaps some fringe authors like Wettan-Kleinbaum (1983) in conjunction with other sources listed in the bibliography will of course be taken into account when comparing their stories of the Amazons' way of life to the modern discoveries in the digs. We shall also be looking at some Internet (IN) sites listed in the bibliography, both of a genuine research nature and some of those that cater to women who appear to be desperate to find a niche in life and who try to emulate their heroes, the Amazon Warriors of old.

So I think that first we should look at the ancient legends themselves and possibly how they were used by the playwrights of Ancient Athens to create characters who would make the establishment gasp, probably with a mixture of wonder and fury that women could even be thought to be on a par with the men. The vase paintings and sculptures of amazonomachy and others, many of which come from the pediment of the Parthenon, illustrate quite a few of the legends and could maybe allow us to see how the Amazons were thought of by the ancient Athenians. If we then investigate the findings of modern archaeology, we can attempt to find out if there is any sort of correlation that would enable us to say the Amazons did exist, rather than simply tribes of warrior women for whom there is considerable evidence.

Chapter 2

Legends of the Amazons

Perhaps the first thing we should do is to look at some tales of the Amazons and how they fitted in with other characters from Greek myth and legend. The reason for doing so is simply to see if their legends sit comfortably with those of Achilles, Theseus, and Herakles and to try to decide if there is a tension there that will not allow a comfortable fit.

Tales of the Amazon warriors are many and varied, from their lifestyle to the battles they fought and the Greek heroes who fought against them. Although there were in general several versions of each of the Greek myths, the most popular according to Greek legend was that the Amazons were the children of Ares, the God of War, and a Naiad called Harmonia. However, others think that their mother was Aphrodite, the mother of Ares. Perhaps this was an indication that the Amazons were seen as an inseparable dichotomy of love and war, although with love taking a poor second place. In Greek mythology, Amazons were from either a legendary nation of women warriors or a land of women at the extremities of the known world. It is possible that there is a grain of fact in warrior women among the Scythian nation, which we will come to in due course.

The name Amazon has often been said to derived from the Greek a + mazos, meaning without a breast and traditionally, Hellanikos of Lesbos (c. 480–400 BC) attempted to explain the name by saying that they cauterised the right breast to stop it growing so that it would not interfere with spear throwing or shooting arrows. If we remember that the Greeks associated the left side of the body with femininity and the right side with masculinity, we can possibly appreciate the idea more clearly. However, I do not think this is a viable explanation when we consider that women from other cultures also used bows and arrows, yet the story of removing a breast is applied only to the Amazons. The Mongol women of today are as good as any other female archers and yet they see no need to have a breast removed. As well as that, modern Western female archers have not followed suit. They have retained their body parts and have had considerable success in Olympic competition, so there appears to be no reason as to why the Amazons would mutilate themselves, quite apart from the fact that mutilation would serve no useful purpose whatsoever when attempting to feed their baby daughters and possibly also their sons until weaned. Also, in the sculptures and illustrations, which we can see on various items of pottery, all of the Amazons are shown with both breasts, usually with at least one of them peeping out. The name Amazon is also shrouded in mystery because there are probably as many derivations of the name as there are languages.

"In the case of the females they seared the right breast that it might not project when their bodies matured and be in the way; and it is for this reason that the nation of the Amazons received the appellation it bears" (Diodorus Siculus, Book II, 45,46—General History of the Amazons).

However, another possibility is that the word could be derived from the Iranian ha-mazan, originally meaning warriors, but it seems that no real confirmed etymology is known.

However that may be, the basic facts say that the legendary Amazons appear to have been a nomadic tribe, or tribes, of female warriors who lived without men most of the time. They were horseback warriors armed with bows and arrows and labrys (double headed axes similar to those found in the Palace of Knossos on Crete) as well as their javelins. In the earliest illustrations they appear to be wearing what looks like hoplite armour: a helmet, round shield, sword, and spear. In some cases they wear greaves and a breastplate, but in general their dress varied somewhat over the years, from helmets and short kilts with girdles, which left their legs free and unencumbered in battle to, in the later vase paintings, the barbarian Persian/Oriental style garments with pointed caps with ear flaps (kidaris) and loose leggings, as shown in the frontispiece to Tyrrell, 1984. Both styles are very well illustrated in this line drawing taken from an Attic red figure cup presently housed in Naples.

It is well known that the Athenians kept a force of Scythian slaves as policemen as we note in "Thesmophoriazusae" by Aristophanes, and interestingly, there is an illustration by Epiktetos of a Scythian archer in which the archer is dressed very much like the person on the right in Figure 2. An illustration of this can be seen in Boardman's Athenian Red Figure Vases, plate 77. The Scythian link to the Amazons appears to be somewhat reinforced, although having said that, we should realise that this may reflect Athenian perceptions rather than reality. Also, we should remember that the Persian/Oriental style of dress in the vase paintings may well have been inspired by the final defeat of the Persians by the Greeks at the Battle of Plataea in 479 BC

Figure 2. Two types of Amazon dress. Redrawn from an Attic red-figure cup, *Museo Nationale*, Naples.

and so the Greeks may well have conflated Amazons and Persians, maybe because both were soundly defeated and therefore could possibly have been used interchangeably. They were both regarded as effeminate enemies regardless of their origin, and so it is probably not very surprising that in the fifth century defeating Amazons was at least as popular as defeating the Persian barbarians. In fact, the Amazons, like the kentaurs and any other barbarians such as the Persians only existed to be defeated.

There are illustrations on many other vases, however, as can be seen on a hydria by Hypsis of around 510 BC. This is, at the present, in Munich, at the Antiken-sammlungen (Image number AS 2423). Another held in the Museo Publico in Arrezzo presents a contrast of both styles of dress that can be clearly seen in these two illustrations and again the oriental style is well represented. Herodotus (Book 4, 110) tells us of the Sauromatians, a nomadic tribe who he says were the descendants of the Amazons and the Scythians. After a war between the Greeks and Amazons at the River Thermodon, which the Greeks won, the Amazon captives were put aboard three ships to be taken as slaves to Greece, but when at sea the Greeks were quickly overpowered and killed. Unfortunately the Amazons could not steer or navigate the ship and were cast up on the shores of Scythia, which was an area around the north coast of the modern Black Sea inhabited in ancient times by Iranian nomads. The most significant of these tribes mentioned in Greek sources were located in the area between the Dnieper and Don rivers. When they landed on the coast and moved inland some way, the Amazons found horses grazing, which they seized, and settled down to their normal way of life until the Scythians, who replaced the Cimmerians, at one time masters of the south Russian steppes, discovered them and a fight developed.

At first, the Scythians thought they were fighting men, but when they checked the bodies of the fallen and found them to be women, the Scythians called off the fighting and stayed at some distance from the women. Eventually, one of the younger men came upon a young Amazon warrior as she went apart from the others to relieve herself. He made advances, and she allowed him to have sex with her, so we know that they were not immune to the lure of sexual desire. On parting, she made it known by signing that he was to bring a friend with him the next day and she would bring one of her friends. The Scythians themselves had something of a reputation for their mastery of the bow and arrow, and so they worked well with their Amazon counterparts. The men could not learn the women's language, but the women succeeded in picking up the men's so when they could understand each other, the Scythians made the following proposal: "We," they said, "have parents and property. Let us give up our present way of life and return to live with our people. We will keep you as our wives and not take any others." The Amazons replied, "We and the women of your nation could never live together; our ways are too much at variance. We are riders; our business is with the bow and spear, and we know nothing of women's work. But in your country no woman has anything to do with such things—your women stay at home in their wagons occupied with feminine tasks, and never go out to hunt or for any other purpose. We could not possibly agree. If, however, you wish to keep us for your wives and to behave as honourable men, go out and get from your parents the share of property, which is due to you, and then let us go off and live by ourselves" (Herodotus 4. 110 ff.).

So the romances, for want of a better description, blossomed until finally at the prompting of the Amazons, the young Scythian men requested their share of the family possessions, upon which both Scythians and Amazons left to form their own village, some six days travel to the north-east of the original location at Lake Maeotis (Herodotus, The Histories, 110–111). According to Herodotus, this was the beginning of the Sauromatian race and in his day, these women were hunters and fighters who rode and fought alongside their menfolk. Another point we should note here is that they had a law that said they could not marry until they had killed a man in battle. In this scenario then, men and women rode and fought together, not like the legends that say that the Amazons were loners who lived apart from the men.

The first author, although he said little enough, to really introduce the Amazons was Homer, when he wrote the *Iliad*, the story of the Trojan War, which, if it did in fact take place at all, would traditionally have been around 1185 BC. Unfortunately, he was writing roughly four hundred years after the event and only from hearsay, from stories that had come down through the years. Accuracy must therefore be extremely suspect. Although not mentioned by Homer the epic cycle tells us that King Priam, in his later years, was assisted against the Greeks by the Amazon Queen Penthesilea and her warriors. She, however, was slain by Achilles who, we are told, promptly fell in love with her dead body and was accused by Thersites of necrophilia. Partially because Thersites is supposed to have struck a blow to the eye of Penthesilea as she lay dying, Achilles took grave exception to this further insult with the result that Thersites met his doom very quickly. Penthesilea's corpse was subsequently given back to the Trojans for burial. Of course, there is always another version of the story, and Diktys of Crete's version is that her dying body was dragged to the banks of the River Scamandros and thrown into it by Diomedes.

According to Diodorus Siculus, this all came about because Queen Penthesilea had apparently shot and killed her sister Hippolyte accidentally whilst out hunting for deer and had gone to Priam for absolution. When that was forthcoming, she and her warriors stayed on out of gratitude to offer their aid. There are other variations that depend upon whose account we read. Hellanikos of Lesbos said that Penthesilea was a combatant at Troy so that she could kill her quota of men and be permitted to marry. This is because some stories are told that Amazon women must have a number of kills (Herodotus, as already mentioned, says that "No girl shall wed until they have killed a man in battle," but others mention up to about five kills) to their credit before they can marry. The

Figure 3. Achilles killing Queen Penthesilea. Exekias black-figure painting, 540-530 BC, British Museum.

number of kills varies from source to source. As we have been told, Penthesilea and her warriors performed magnificently, but unfortunately she was killed on the battlefield by Achilles, who, as I have mentioned, displayed a grave weakness by falling in love with her. Quintus of Smyrna (fourth century AD) had access to earlier, now lost, writings when he wrote his description of Queen Penthesilea's part in the Trojan War and his description of her death at the hands of Achilles. This story is illustrated in several vase paintings, such as the one presently housed in the British Museum (Figure 3). This is a wine jar, made in Athens about 540–530 BC (Vase B 210) and is a black-figure painting by Exekias, originally found at Vulci in Italy.

Myths and legends were fair game for the vase painters who were always on the lookout for themes to help them sell vases and utensils of various types. The Amazons made an ideal subject, probably partially because of the emotive appeal and also because of the large amount of material available. There are many stories about the Amazons and heroes from Greek legend that were passed on by word of mouth and the imaginations of the artists who put flesh on the bones of the stories for the considerable number of people who could not read. Although the poorer people could not afford to purchase these cups, plates, and other decorated items, at least they could see and enjoy the stories in pictures painted on them, which they had been told about by their parents and grandparents. The pictures on the vases and the sculptures gave life to the legends that came from a much earlier Greece. The illustrations were a way of keeping traditional stories alive in the minds of uneducated people and for onward transmission to their children and grand-children.

We should not forget that we in the twenty-first century AD owe a great deal to the imaginations of the vase painters and other artists, because, apart from illustrating the legends themselves, the pictures have given us a tremendous amount of information about daily life and customs in ancient Greece, especially Athens. Some of the illustrations actually show the interiors of potters' workshops, and the techniques involved in loading the kiln, firing, and decorating the pots (Phoca, 1992). The book also contains a Potters' Hymn, in which they ask Athena to protect their work from the destructive evil spirits Syntrips (Smasher), Smaragos (Roarer), Asbatos (Unquenchable), Sabaktes (Shatterer), and Omodamos (Conqueror of the Unbaked) who apparently sneaked into the kiln and were blamed for breakages in firing. Without the illustrations on the vases we could only guess at many details that are quite obvious in the illustrations and vase paintings, and so we should be very grateful for the artists' excellent and very useful custom of very often identifying, in the main, the figures involved in the different scenes. We should also remember that many people claimed descent from the gods and the early heroes and those people claiming this ancestry helped to create and maintain a ready market for the output from the potters, vase painters, and sculptors. The pottery also provided an important economic benefit to, not only Athens, but in the early days Corinth before her decline, and later Magna Graecia (Southern Italy) as well. Many vases were produced in Southern Italy where all of the vases with scenes from the theatre originated, since the Athenian style was simply illustrating myths, legends, and scenes from daily life.

Amazonomachy was a very popular theme in Attic black-figure vase paintings—the earliest Herakles versus the Amazons dates from the seventh century BC. There are also many sculptures of amazonomachy (battles with Amazons) that helped to tell the stories and support the information in the paintings. Some of these sculptors, as well as those depicting kentauromachy and gigantomachy, are from the pediment of the Acropolis. Some of the main themes, apart from those of Herakles, were the stories surrounding Theseus, who became King of Athens and one of its foremost heroes. This, of course, was after his father Aegeus killed himself because he mistakenly thought that Theseus had been killed by the Minotaur. The arrangement made with his father was that after he had despatched the Minotaur, Theseus was to change the black sails of his ship to white so that Aegeus would know that he had triumphed. Alas, Theseus in his triumph forgot to change the sails, and so Aegeus thought that his son and the hostages had perished whereby he jumped off the cliff and perished himself. Many are the tales of Theseus and his exploits, including his capture and rape of Hippolyte (or possibly Antiope), one of the Amazon queens. Again, as in so many other stories, which have been told and re-told, we have the theme of Athenian male dominance, especially over the Amazons, whose way of life was at such odds to that of Athenian women in general. There is a cup in the British Museum (GR 1850.3-2.3, Vases E 84, attributed to the Kodros painter from c. 430 BC) that depicts the exploits of Theseus around the outside. On the tondo is a scene of Theseus dragging the dead or dying Minotaur from the labyrinth, which is suggested by the meander around the entrance. Many more scenes from Ancient Greece can be seen on the British Museum website, www.britishmuseum.org.

After the Amazons had conquered almost all of Asia, they invaded Athens to punish Theseus for carrying away Antiope either by force or voluntarily and were in turn conquered by Theseus. Antiope was a sister of Hippolyte and some authors would say that Theseus married Hippolyte, from which union was born the son Hippolytus, around whom Euripides formed his play, set in the days when Theseus had married Phaedra after his divorce from Hippolyte (or her death). Theoretically, chastity was a virtue not found among the Greek men, only among the women, but Hippolytus was cast as a virginal woman hater, a "soft" man who could not contribute to either family or state and who had time only for Artemis Parthenos, the virgin huntress and goddess of virginity. Aphrodite was her polar extreme as the goddess of license and of eros and most certainly, he had little time for Aphrodite, which made her quite angry and rather vengeful. She it was who instigated the cry of rape from Phaedra and was thus the direct cause of Theseus killing his own son. So, by extension, not only the Amazons themselves were put down, but their offspring as well. Euripides here and with his character Aeschylus in his Oresteia provides us with a comparison between a lady-man and a strong woman like Clytemnestra to illustrate how much damage can be caused by such a woman. The message here seems to be that female sexuality can destroy man and is therefore something to be feared and defeated wherever it is found. However, female sexuality is not the whole story. I rather suspect that the main problem that the Greeks had was more to do with female intelligence. Think about all of the Greek heroes who were aided by women to achieve their ends—does it not cause you to wonder what the Greek men could have achieved had the women been one hundred per cent behind them? And more to the point, would the Greek warriors listen to them? Perhaps this is what Aristophanes was trying to highlight in his "Ekklesiazusae."

Women had to be properly controlled so that they could not create havoc, especially in family life like Medea's in which she murdered her two sons. The old saying that "Hell hath no fury like a woman scorned" is certainly true of Medea. She was put to one side by Jason after she helped him, at the expense of the loss of her own family to obtain the Golden Fleece from Colchis, in order for him to take a new politically advantageous wife, the daughter of Cleon. Having said that, Medea is an example of a heroic barbarian woman, as Jason several times labelled her, (barbarian, not heroic). He was not very complimentary when he told her that she had left a barbarous land to come to a much more up-market country. He also called her a Tuscan Scylla, a barbarian by another name. She took determined control of her own life and certainly seemed to have every sympathy with the Amazons, at least as far as marriage was concerned. In her famous speech, Medea seems to have had a problem with the fact that the women had to buy a husband with their dowry, but she was much more upset with the fact that the husband actually became their master in law. She was most definitely not amused. I should think that could be pretty much how the Amazons would have felt.

Herakles, one of the best-known Greek heroes, had to perform twelve labours assigned to him by Eurystheus son of Sthenelos. After Herakles recovered from a attack of insanity in which he killed his children, he was advised by the Oracle at Delphi to serve Eurystheus for a period of twelve years and perform any labours required by him, after which he would become immortal. Herakles was a popular figure in sculpture, in vase painting, and ceramics cast in heroic mould, all of which show some of his labours and his fights against various Amazon warriors. Unfortunately, he was also lampooned as a figure of fun, as a gourmand with a big mouth, gargantuan appetite, and a loud roar. In Aristophanes' play "Frogs" he lent his lion skin and club to Dionysus, who turned out to be a trembling coward when on an adventure to the Underworld in order to bring back the greatest dramatist to the surface again (Either Euripides or Aeschylus). Both Herakles and Theseus are said to have raped Amazons, thereby ensuring that the females were humbled. Herakles' ninth labour was to obtain the Golden Zôstêr (belt or girdle) of Ares from Hippolyte in order that Eurystheus could present it to his daughter Admete (Apollodorus ii, 5). He was accompanied on this venture by his friend Theseus, who carried off Antiope, Hippolyte's sister and thus prompted a retaliatory invasion of Athens by the rest of the Amazon tribe. Herakles' popularity as a major opponent of the Amazons began to wane as Theseus and the Athenians took over the running.

The Anatolian Amazons (those who lived on the Asian side of the Bosporus) helped inspire the Thermodontine (from the European side) Amazons' signature accessory, the belt. This belt was given to her by her mother and was a symbol of independence and the fact that she was her own mistress, belonging to no man. The zôstêr (belt) of the Amazons could possibly have served a dual function in that at the very basic and practical level it could simply have been a protective device which covered the reproductive organs, but it could also have been a symbol of partheneia (virginity). The taking of the zôstêr of Hippolyte could well have been a euphemism for the taking of her virginity, whether by rape or voluntarily given. Hippolyte, Antiope, and Melanippe were the three Amazon queens who reigned at the time when Herakles visited them at Themiskyra. According to Graves (1960, 488f), Hippolyte offered her zôstêr to Herakles because she was attracted to his muscular body. However, because of the trickery of Hera in which she disguised herself and went among the Amazons saying that Herakles had come to kidnap their queen, the Amazons warriors were outraged and promptly attacked. In the heat of the moment Herakles unfortunately killed Hippolyte and took the zôstêr. Another version of this story by Apollonius of Rhodes was that Herakles kidnapped Melanippe, daughter of the queen, and then ransomed her unharmed for the zôstêr (Argonautica II, 966–969). Another item held by the Museo Publico is a kantharos on which there is a painting of Herakles fighting Amazons (Figure 4) painted by Douris around 490 BC.

But there are quite a few other adventures of Herakles shown on a series of vases, such as the fight with the Cretan bull and that against the Nemean lion as well as his fights with other gods like Apollo, whom he fought for a deer and in a different painting, a tripod. Some scenes show Herakles actually working with another god or goddess like Athena, but in general most scenes are of Herakles fighting someone or something. Many of the paintings and sculptures involve Herakles and Amazon warriors, in all of which Herakles triumphs. Again, we have the Greek victory against the Amazons— another one of so many victories that one may well wonder how the Amazons could continue to exist against all the odds.

Figure 4. Herakles fighting Amazon warriors. From a
kantharos by Douris, c.490BC.

Tales of the Amazons and their defeats at the hands of
the Greeks seem to have been used as salutary lessons to
upper class Athenian wives in an attempt to make them
more amenable to their husband's wishes. The Greek
men certainly did not accept that there was anything positive about the Amazon society but treated it all with
great negativity. Their attitudes were most certainly not
the means to empower women. In fact, the pictures on
either side of an epinetron housed in the Louvre museum
demonstrate this admirably. The epinetron was bell-
shaped with one half of it cut away so that it would sit on
the knee of the Greek women when working with wool.
The illustration on one side of the tool was of upper class
Greek women chatting quite merrily whilst working. The
other side, however, depicts a group of Amazons prepar-

ing for battle. They are very different pictures and present quite a contrast between the two cultures. One side represents the feminine ideal of the Athenians and the other a cautionary tale of the horrors to come should the women become like the Amazons and unravel the social structure of the times. It may well be that the customary segregation of the Athenian men and women and the male fear of the female sexuality or intelligence have something to do with this attitude. Illustrations of the pictures on each side of the epinetron may be seen at www.wisc.edu/arth/ah301/23-women/37.image.html.

The message may also have been as much for the men themselves in order to uphold the ideology that they were the dominant species and to warn that withdrawal from normal family life would be very detrimental to the fabric of society as a whole. The Amazons were a complete gender reversal for the male Athenians when one considers that the Athenian upper class women stayed at home and looked after the very heart of Athenian patriarchy, the oikos and the children, after having borne them. Their education was confined to the domestic practices of their times. They could not own property and while a man could divorce his wife by eviction, she had to enlist a male relative to petition the court on her behalf. They had little or no freedom from male dominance, since it would appear that the Greeks could not envisage a society in which men and women were equal partners and able to offer mutual support, working together as equal partners. To the Greek male, a woman could not be an equal partner, nor was she her own person.

In Homer's Odyssey, Telemachus, son of Odysseus, claimed total authority over the oikos for himself. He told his mother Penelope to mind her own woman's work and go back to her spinning and weaving thus leaving him to address the unruly suitors in the absence of Odysseus himself. There was a clearly defined polarity between the men and women in ancient Greece. The Greek male had a view of his own society, and somewhat like fairly modern attitudes towards children everything was well when the children were quiet and out of sight. It was almost as though the Greeks somehow feared having women as equals and allowing them to have an equal say, whereas the Amazons controlled marriage, essentially by refusing to have anything to do with it. They had no inclination to be bound by society and the bonds of matrimony, and they stood out as a permanent sore thumb of the city society.

Since the Amazons had already achieved what the Greeks aspired to, i.e., they already had become warriors, the Greek male felt threatened. Unlike the Amazons who made their own way in the world, Greek women only became part of adult society by providing their husband with a son and not simply by marrying into society. So the Greeks felt that it was unnatural for women not to be dominated by the men and not to provide sons to continue the family and race. The Amazons had children certainly, but they valued only the females—a total reversal from the Greeks, who practised exposure of new-born baby girls, much the same as the way in which Atalanta was abandoned as an infant by her father. To put it in simple terms, Greeks valued males and de-valued females. The Amazons were completely opposite.

Many of the Greek tragic authors used this gender difference to great effect as we have mentioned, but Aristophanes was not above poking fun at the whole idea of reversal in order to win competitions at the

Lenaia and the Great Dionysia. In "Ekklesiazusae" the women dress as men, steal their clothes, wear false beards, and sneak off to the Assembly in order to take over the running of the polis as their solution to the problems besetting Athens. The women put forward their own solutions based on their own desires and these were adopted by the Assembly. Euripides was lampooned in the "Thesmophoriazusae" when the women at the festival accused him of misogyny. Agathon the playwright appeared dressed as a woman, and Mnesilochus became a cross-dressing hero/heroine, thus using gender as a comic tool. However, the fact that they were written and produced as comedies gives us a clue that perhaps the whole notion of reversal was not to be taken too seriously, although that should not be taken as read. Perhaps the definitive classic example of women taking over from the men is his final anti-war play, "Lysistrata," which was performed in 411 BC after the mad gesture of Athenian ὕβρις (hubris) and their disastrous defeat in Sicily. Although having every appearance of a comedy with the attendant sexual jokes and crude humour this, however, may have been a sincere attempt by Aristophanes, a cry from the heart, so to speak, to put a halt to the Athenian headlong rush towards disaster, which finally took place in 404 BC after their comprehensive defeat by the Spartans. In "Lysistrata" Aristophanes cast Spartans instead of Amazons, whom the Athenians could not relate to in the same way. The point in this, of course, is that he did not cast anyone as an Amazon warrior, but preferred to use Spartan women instead. Athens and Sparta were often at loggerheads with each other, and so he may well have felt that it was a topical idea that most Athenians could relate to, rather than introduce distant enemies who were not on the

Athenian doorstep and who could not pose an immediate threat. So in this play, the Athenian and Spartan women, as well as Boeotian, Megaran, and Acharnians, came together as allies and refused to contemplate the fulfilment of their sexual role led, of course, by the Athenian "Lysistrata" (She who Disbands Armies), in order to highlight the futility of war and the public feeling against it.

By having the Acropolis and Treasury invaded and taken over by the old women, he is also drawing a parallel with the Amazons of old when they occupied part of Athens, the Areopagus. This happened when Theseus was King of Athens and either abducted or persuaded, depending upon which account you read, the Amazon princess Antiope to return to Athens with him. When the Amazons invaded in 490 BC in order to return her to her people there was a stand-off for some time because, for whatever reason, Theseus was reluctant to attack them. After he had performed a sacrifice to Fear, the battle was joined with Theseus and the Athenians eventually winning after a series of battles lasting for several months in total. The final victory came when Theseus defeated the Amazons before the Acropolis itself. This does, however, show how warlike and how efficient as soldiers the Amazons were, because even the Persians and all their armies did not get any farther than Marathon in 490 BC. Not for another ten years did the Persians get as far as the Amazons had. Although in a contradiction to the practice of reclaiming the dead after a battle according to the Greek stories, the Amazons died on the retreat from Athens and they were buried by the wayside. The problem with this scenario is that it was considered unlucky to bury the dead within the city walls, and so Athenians were buried alongside the same road. Perhaps they gave up their resting places to an influx of Amazon warriors and so became unknown themselves. Amazon tombs are said to be found at Megara, Athens, and Chalcis, amongst other places and Amazon shrines were supposed to have been located at Athens and Chalcis. This of course implied the presence of a tomb and probably also a cult, since there were annual sacrifices to the Amazons on the day before the Thesea at Athens. Unfortunately, like so many others, this is something of a bald statement, with no flesh on its bones and gives us no idea who could have been involved in the sacrifice.

However, Plutarch also mentions the sacrifices at a place called the Horcomosium adjoining the Theseum, so one would assume that the sacrifices were carried out by the Athenians themselves, just prior to the annual festival of Theseus. Before the Thesea the Athenians offered sacrifice to the Amazons, thus commemorating the victory of Theseus over the women. All fourteen of the west metopes are badly preserved, but are generally thought to be amazonomachies that show a fairly balanced contest between the Greeks and the Amazons. Enough fragments of the east pedimental sculpture have been discovered to recover the theme, the apotheosis of Herakles. The frieze contains sculptures only in the metopes of the east front and in those of the sides immediately adjoining it; the frontal metopes represent the labours of Herakles, the lateral the exploits of Theseus. The eastern frieze represents a battle scene with seated deities on either hand, the western one a kentauromachia (battle between Greeks and kentaurs). The information about the Theseum from Plutarch, though, is somewhat sketchy and no reasons for or details of the ceremony are given by him, most likely because when Plutarch wrote about this there would have been no need to explain it because none of the Athenian citizens would have required any explanations.

There were major differences in upbringing between the Spartan and Athenian women. For example, the Spartan women were given better food to eat and encouraged to train with the men in order to keep themselves fit—for childbearing reasons mostly. Lysistrata's opposite number from Sparta was Lampito, a clear example of how the Spartan women were encouraged to be. Lysistrata, on the arrival of Lampito congratulates her on looking so pretty and fit. The fact that Lysistrata thought she could strangle a bull is an indication of fitness. Lampito puts her fitness down to a workout in the gym every day, and to the kordax, a form of Spartan dance in which their feet came in contact with their posteriors on a very regular basis. This standard of fitness was expected of Spartan women and Amazons alike. The Athenians, however, saw no reason to allow that sort of freedom to their women or that they should be fit for childbirth.

Although the Spartans married, promiscuity was, if not actively encouraged, turned a blind eye to—even to the extent of a husband lending his wife to another Spartan citizen for the purpose of procreation, because considerable numbers of the Spartan men were very often off fighting somewhere. At least this way the women could continue to provide fodder for the army. Spartan women were, if you like, a sort of half-way house between the Athenians and Amazons, as far removed from one as they were the other, with one possible exception. The Spartans raised all of their female children in a fashion similar to that of the Amazons, but the male children had to be examined to find out if they were fit to become warriors and only the fittest were kept (Pomeroy, 36). Pomeroy does not explain what happened to those who did not make the grade, although exposure or being given to their father were the likely outcomes. The Spartan women did have some features in common with the Amazons, like the fact that Artemis was the patron of both the Spartans and the Amazons. So if we were to pose a question, "was Sparta influenced by Amazon women," it could well be a very valid one. Another point to consider is that on her wedding night, the Spartan woman was clothed only in a simple shift fastened by a belt. This belt was removed by the new husband as a prelude to further celebration and intimacies and was again, a reference to the parthenos state symbolised by a belt, or girdle. Perhaps the Spartans created their view of women from stories that they heard about how the Amazons protected their territory, or maybe Lycurgus was inspired to raise the status of Spartan women, being influenced by the stories he had heard. I think it unlikely that the Amazons were their forebears, but it is possible that they had some influence. Like the Greeks of Athens, the Spartan men feared feminine power and as Cartledge (2002, 161/2) would have it, an expression of the male Greek fear was the invention of the Amazon race on which to focus their fear, perhaps even a phobia of feminine power. The "mythical" aspect we shall consider later, when we examine the archaeological remains found in Russia, Georgia, and the Southern Ukraine by modern archaeologists such as Dr. Davis-Kimball et al.

Chapter 3

Location of the Amazons

There are those (Tyrrell, 1984) who consider that the Greeks invented this mythological race of warrior women, the Amazons. The reasons for them doing so seem to be pretty much that the Greeks needed a focus for their nationalistic pride, someone or something that they could praise and in so doing, praise themselves. There is also the thought that the Athenians required a "comfort factor or zone" and so the Amazons were invented to show all that was wrong with the non-Athenian way of life. They, in fact, became a concrete manifestation of the ills that beset Athens and as such must be, and would be seen to be conquered.

But what of the myth of the Amazons? Were they simply that, a myth, or is there any basis in fact for their existence? To search for an answer this question we must turn to modern archaeology and consider the findings in regions of Southern Russia, Georgia, and the Ukraine by people such as Professor Rolle and Dr. Davis-Kimball, among others. It could be an advantage for us to consider when and where the Amazons existed, if in fact they did, and so we will first have a look at when the Amazons were written about and try to place them in time. Once we have an idea of when they were, we can consider their place, or places in space and maybe find out whether modern research can support the notion of warrior women, Amazon or not.

Homer probably composed the *Iliad* sometime in the eighth Century BC. It deals with the Trojan War and tells about the battles between the Greeks and Trojans outside the walls of Troy, including the heroics of Achilles and Hector. In it, Homer refers to the Amazons as antianeira, "Those who fight like men," or possibly meaning "hostile to men" and later, in the fifth century BC, Herodotus calls them androktones, "killers of men." Herodotus also tells us that the Scythians called them oiorpata, "man-killers."

In Book III of the *Iliad* King Priam of Troy remembers the time when, as a young man some years prior to the Trojan War he was assisting the Phrygians against attack and "that time the Amazons, who fight like men, came up to attack." From this we can infer that the Amazons were around in mythical times at least two generations before the battle for Troy. When we think about Heinrich Schliemann discovering the ruins of Troy in the mid-nineteenth century, we have to remember that a possible date of the Battle for Troy is in the region of 1185 BC, although not all scholars agree that there actually was a battle at all. Looking at the Ancient History Time Line in (IN Ref 28), we can see that at the entry for 1200 BC doubt is cast on whether there ever was a Trojan War. Homer was not writing until around four hundred years after the event and was relying on ancient stories that had been passed down by word of mouth. We must therefore treat his stories of Amazon warriors with a certain amount of scepticism until, or more likely if, his writings on the subject can either be proved or disproved. We also run into a similar problem with the writings of Herodotus from the fifth century BC. He too is relying on traditional stories from the past, and it was assumed for some time that Herodotus' information was unreliable. However, modern archaeology has provided, if not proof exactly, a certain amount of support for his information about the nomads, their lives, and their burial customs, which he recorded during his travels. But who knows how much they may have changed in the time between Homer and Herodotus? Even the myths and legends finally entrusted to writing must remain somewhat suspect because of errors in copying them and differences in translation.

Herodotus recounts a story about a warrior queen Tomyris, who ruled the Massagetae in the sixth century BC. The story is of a battle between Tomyris and Cyrus the Great, founder of the Persian Empire, who attempted to annex her territory into the Achaemenid Empire. The Massagetae won the battle, but because Tomyris' son took his own life after being taken prisoner. Tomyris searched the battlefield for the body of Cyrus. She found it and removed his head, which she put into a skin filled with human blood because she had threatened Cyrus with giving him his fill of blood. Cyrus had taken over from his father Cambyses I in about 558 BC as king of the Persians. He was a humane and enlightened ruler, but unfortunately he was killed in the battle with the Massagetae, who in their turn, were defeated by his son Cambyses II. So far, we seem to be looking at dates for the Amazons between about 1200 BC and 400 BC, but Diodorus Siculus tells us about Libyan Amazons who preceded the Amazons mentioned in the Greek legends. In his Book III, 52–55, we are told that "the majority of mankind believe that the only Amazons were those who are reported to have dwelt in the neighbourhood of the Thermodon River on the Pontus; but the truth is otherwise, since the Amazons of Libya were much earlier in point of time." He goes further and says that "This race of Amazons disappeared entirely many generations before the Trojan War, whereas the women about the Thermodon River were in their full vigour a little before that time" (Diodorus Siculus, Book III Section 52).

There is also information to the effect that Amazons may have populated the island of Lemnos in the north Aegean Sea in the third millennium BC, but unfortunately the evidence seems to be entirely circumstantial. If this could be proven, we would have a four millennia old race of women warriors, but I should think that this proof is rather unlikely to be forthcoming in the foreseeable future, if ever. Recent finds on the island of Lemnos shows up some similarities in Greek mythology between the Amazons and the Argonauts who found this island inhabited only by women. The Argonauts named the island as γυναικοκρατουμενε (ruled by women). The women, ruled by Hypsipyle, had killed all of their husbands and welcomed the Argonauts with open arms because of the heavy work only the men could do. The men initially pitched in with a will, but eventually suspicions began to be aroused. Jason then called the men together and reminded them of their mission whereupon they set sail to continue on their way to Colchis.

An interesting link between Lemnos and the Amazons of Greek mythology is that an ancient city called Myrina on Lemnos has the same name as one of the early Amazon queens. The archaeology on Lemnos includes finds of arrowheads, battle axes, and delicate tools, which have "obviously" been used for cosmetic purposes. Why "obviously" is not explained. Simply because the Amazons are said to have used bows and arrows and battle axes, there seems to have been rather a large leap made in saying that Amazons must have lived on Lemnos. Comparisons have been made between buildings on Lemnos and at Thermodon, again making a basic, and in all likelihood, erroneous assumption that Amazons did actually exist simply because of similarities in the methods of building, but this is a report from the Amazon Research Network and unfortunately no author has claimed responsibility for this information or provided any references for the information contained in the report. This does make it a little difficult to assess its veracity and accuracy. While I personally find the website interesting, accepting everything that is written there without question could be somewhat misleading since the report appears to be a particularly subjective one without the benefit of any supporting evidence.

Considering the foregoing, we can now extend the dates of the Amazons, although not all are the Classical Amazon warriors, from 1200 BC, well past 400 BC right up to the present day. If we also take into consideration the Lemnian and the Libyan Amazons which Diodorus Siculus mentions in the first century BC, this time-span may possibly be increased even more, from the third millennium BC to the present day, although the evidence for the earlier ones is not compelling.

Having now achieved some sense of time when the Amazons were supposed to have lived, the next step is to try to define where they lived and had their cities, if indeed they had any. Attempting to locate the Amazons in any particular area is no easier than trying to date them. In the epic cycle Amazons are located in an undefined area of Northern Anatolia beyond Troy. Scythia also figured as a possible site for the Amazons, and as time passed, the location of their homelands gradually moved north-westwards to the northern coast of the Black Sea. It was not until the fifth century that a completely different site was put forward as the homelands of the Amazons—Themiskyra on the River Thermodon, on the southern coast of the Black Sea. The earliest literary reference to Themiskyra as the home of the Amazons is in the Prometheus Vinctus (721–728), in which Prometheus describes the migration of the Amazons from the North to Themiskyra opposite. According to Schwab the River Thermodon rose from a mountainous spring and soon afterwards it split into a great number of branches. The number of these branches was so great that it needed only four more to reach a hundred. He said that the Amazons dwelt at the mouth of the widest outlet, but he also said that they did not all live in the one city and were scattered all over the countryside in separate tribes (Schwab, 1947, 102). However, "The Amazons then, as they appear in the Homeric poems, are a horde of warrior women who strive against men, and with whom conflict is dangerous even to the bravest of heroes. They belong to Asia Minor, seemingly at home in the neighbourhood of Lycia and opponents of the Phrygians on the river Sangarius" (Bennett, 1912, 2).

"It may be concluded that there were three centres to which Greek tradition assigned the Amazons: one in western Asia Minor, a large district in the form of a strip stretching from the Propontis to the tip of Lycia; the second in Pontus along the Euxine, with a western boundary at Sinope, an eastern at Colchis, and a southern undefined, somewhere in the interior of Cappadocia; a third in Scythia, conceived as the Tauric Chersonese, the regions east of Lake Maeotis, those north of the same lake, and probably also those that border the Euxine on the north and west, including Thrace. Each of these is an area so large that only by extension of the term may it be denoted a centre. Threads of affiliation reach out also to

Libya, Egypt, and Syria. Out of this maze the source of the Amazon legend is to be sought" (Bennett, 1912, 12).

"Now in the country along the Thermodon River, as the account goes, the sovereignty was in the hands of a people among whom the women held the supreme power, and its women performed the services of war just as did the men. Of these women one, who possessed the royal authority, was remarkable for her prowess in war and her bodily strength, and gathering together an army of women she drilled it in the use of arms and subdued in war some of the neighbouring peoples. . . . In general, this queen was remarkable for her intelligence and ability as a general, and she founded a great city named Themiskyra at the mouth of the Thermodon River and built there a famous palace" (Diodorus Siculus, Book II, 45, 46). You may be able to see some of the problems which we have in locating the Amazons.

Map 1 indicates the general area that we are talking about. Several authors have written about different tribes living in different areas and of course trying to verify these writings is not the easiest task in the world. However, it is possible that the prototype of the Amazons might have been based on an entirely different source from Scythia or Anatolia, that of the Minoan civilisation of Crete, the forerunner of the mainland Mycenaean and Greek civilisations, but we must bear in mind that legends link them to the Black Sea region rather than Crete. Another offering is that the Amazons were closely associated with Caucasian Albania, which has no relation to modern Albania. It covered most of modern Azerbaijan and had twenty-six tribes including the Gagarians. This name is, of course, familiar as the tribe with which the Amazons we are told, used to dally on an annual basis for the purpose of procreation.

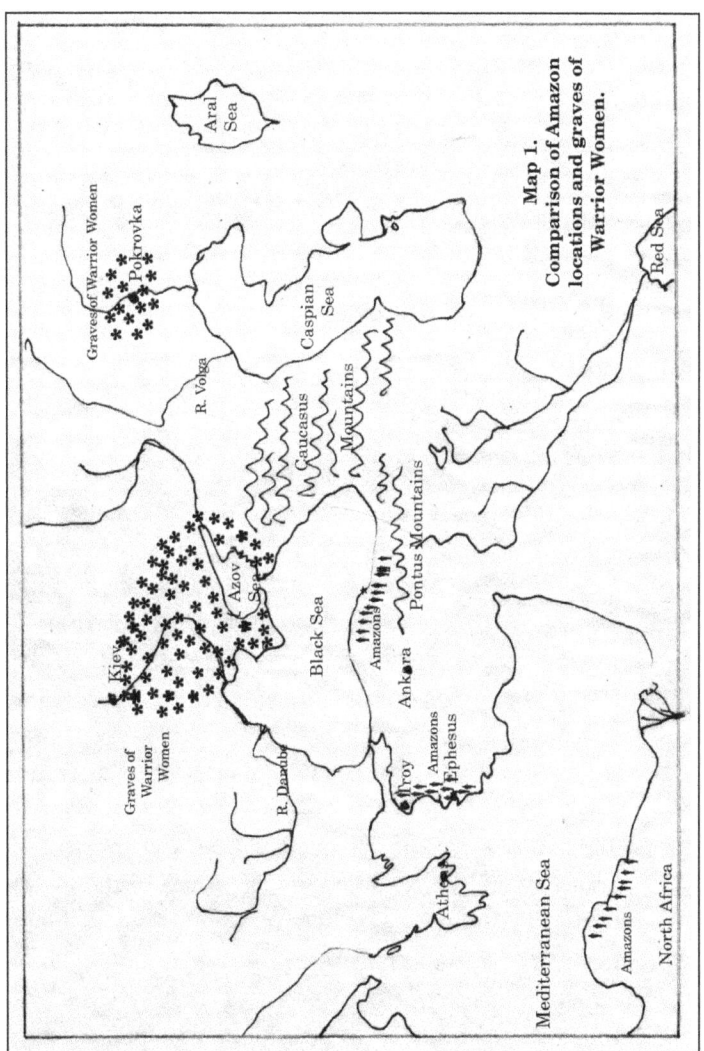

Map 1. Showing the literary locations of the Amazon Warriors and the graves of warrior women.

"In the spring, they celebrate two special months when they climb the nearby mountains, which separate them from the Gagarians. Following an old custom, the Gagarians meet them there and carry out sacrifices with the Amazons. Then they unite to procreate children. They do it secretly in the dark—every Gagarian with the Amazon women that they choose. After the women become pregnant, they return. The female children who are born to the Amazons are kept, but the boys are passed over to the Gagarians to raise. Each Gagarian who is given a child raises it as his own son, despite the uncertainty of its origin."

Dr. Farid Alakbarli, Director of the Department of Information and Translation of the Institute of Manuscripts of the Azerbaijan National Academy of Sciences, is quite definite when he tells us that the Amazons were not a figment of imaginations of the ancient historians. Women warriors existed in the plains of Eurasia and the Ukrainian steppes. He also says that ancient Azerbaijan was known as the Land of the Amazons as well as the Land of Fire. The following internet address will give some more information about that: www.azer.com/aiweb/categories/magazine/ai131_folder/131_articles/131_amazons.html

Perhaps the best known of the Amazons are those who are supposed to have lived at the mouth of the River Thermodon, in their city of Themiskyra. The modern name for the Thermodon is Terme Çay, and it empties into the Black Sea on the northern coast of Turkey (Map 1). The actual site of Themiskyra has not as yet been discovered. Assuming that its historical location is where it is said to be, we can see its supposed location on the map on the south coast of the Black Sea. The Amazons were most probably a nomadic people, so living in a city may not make much sense. It would, though, make more sense were Themiskyra a plain that lay between Chadesia and the Thermodon River and where the Amazons were free to roam at will.

Although in all likelihood nomadic, the Amazons have been credited with the building of the Artemisium, the Temple of Diana of the Ephesians at Ephesus mentioned in the Bible, by Callimachus in his Hymn to Artemis. The Temple of Artemis was located near the ancient city of Ephesus, about fifty kilometres south of the modern Izmir. Nothing remains today of the temple although it was one of the Seven wonders of the Ancient world. Diana of course is the Roman name for Artemis, the goddess of the Amazons, who have also been credited with founding several outposts dotted around the Aegean Sea.

Some people tend to assume that the Amazon race was purely mythical, but others would be prepared to say that they have a historical basis. As mentioned briefly, one of the civilisations postulated as a possible source of the Amazon myth is that of the Minoans of Crete, which reached its height during the second millennium BC. Crete, although some time after the Minoan civilisation vanished, does have some links with Greek mythology, as in the story of Theseus and the Minotaur, for example, and also Theseus is very much associated with the Amazons. There may be nothing to this, but it is an interesting speculation. Farnell & Myres, "Anthropology and the Classics" 138ff, theorized that the Amazons possibly had their roots in the Minoan civilization by drawing attention to previously overlooked similarities between the cultures. According to Myres, the tradition interpreted in the light of evidence furnished by supposed Amazon cults seems to have been very similar and may have originated in Minoan culture. There appears to be some similarities between the two cultures and as the investigation into the Minoan civilisation proceeds, archaeologists are finding more and more similarities and potential links. For example, the Minoans grain supply was supposed to have come from farms on the shores of the Black Sea, which if true, could create another possible link to the Amazons. So far we have not really considered to any great extent the possible influence of the Minoan civilisation.

"In their warlike character the Amazons are reflexes of the Woman whom they worshipped. Like the Warrior Goddess of Asia Minor they carry the battle-axe, and in this they are shown to be closely related to the religion of pre-historic Crete, of which the weapon is the conspicuous symbol. Their other weapon, the bow, is also Cretan. . . . We may believe then that the tradition of the Amazons preserves memories of a time when women held the important place in state and religion in Aegean lands, and that they reflect the goddess of this civilisation" (Bennett, 1912, 75)

Like the Minoan women the Amazon, women had equal access to power, and they had no class distinctions among themselves. Unfortunately, we know of the Minoans only through their art, artefacts, and the Linear B script. Again unfortunately, we do not properly understand their language or their writing in the script named Linear A, which has resisted all attempts at decipherment because we have no idea of the underlying language. Archaeologists such as Evans, Bregen, and Cottrell have been instrumental in highlighting similarities between the Minoans, Spartans, and Amazons, all of whom were the very antithesis of the Greek womenfolk. One of the main reasons behind the thought that there may be a link with the Amazon warriors is that the Minoan civilisation was a thalassocracy, a maritime race, and the men were often away from home for extended periods. This left the women and children to their own devices, thereby encouraging them to take a great deal of interest in running the country, both in secular and religious terms. This could well be the case when we consider that "Minos, according to tradition, was the first person to organise a navy. He controlled the greater part of what is now called the Hellenic Sea, [the modern Aegean]; he ruled over the Cyclades, in most of which he founded the first colonies" (Thucydides, I:4). As Diodorus Siculus says, "They alone held the dominion and commanded, administering all public offices and affairs." But he was not writing of the Minoans—he was writing of the Libyan Amazons, who as we remember, came quite some time before the Thermodontine Amazons. Coincidence maybe, but there surely cannot be many races in which the women held sway in this manner.

Women of the Minoan civilisation would have had much more in common with the Amazons and Spartan women because all of them were very much the opposites of Greek women. Since this was a maritime society, Minoan men seem to have spent a great deal of time at sea and the archaeology of Crete seems to point to the fact that because of this, the women may have been encouraged to become more self reliant. All of the evidence we have to support this is entirely circumstantial, although evidence from other Bronze Age cultures in the Aegean would tend to support it. I suppose it could be argued that the women also had superior legal and social positions, but unfortunately this cannot be proven or substantiated without written evidence. One indication we may have of this is the murals that show the women much larger than the men, who acknowledged the women as they passed each other, but not the other way around. The position of women in Minoan Crete would appear to have been very influential. Since they were allowed to participate in the bull-jumping competitions, it would seem that there was no real segregation from the men's activities. Because the Mother Goddess dominated the Minoan belief, the women would have been heavily involved in the rites and ceremonials of the religion and would have enjoyed a high social standing. The chief priestess especially would have wielded great influence, probably even to the extent of having her own throne room as found at Knossos.

Of the two languages found on Crete, Linear A and Linear B, only Linear B, now known to be a form of early Greek, has been deciphered. The tablets which have been decoded and read consist almost entirely of lists and accounts and have little bearing on the social structure of the time. However, the Linear B tablets also name some of the gods and goddesses who were well known in Classical Greece. The names of Athene, Hera, Zeus, and Poseidon have been identified, as well as some others about whom some doubt remains (Alexiou, 74). For those readers who may be contemplating delving into the realms of Minoan religion, "Minoan Civilization" by Stylianos Alexiou, translated from the Greek by Cressida Ridley, would provide a reasonably good introduction. It is a complicated subject, especially when taking into account the gods and goddesses of other cultures who have been "adopted" by the Greeks, so I think it best left to those authors who have made a study of the subject. Perhaps when Linear A is fully deciphered, we may be rewarded with more information about the religious and social life of the Minoans. At present we may only partially read and understand it through Linear B values. Many sites have yielded Linear A inscriptions, but by far the greatest number have come from Hagia Triada.

The indications are that this was a matriarchal and polytheistic society and the throne room restored by Evans in the palace at Knossos would possibly bear this out if we consider that there was only one throne and speculate that it may have been for the use of the chief priestess alone (Cottrell, 1961, plate 7). This speculation is warranted when we take into consideration the other factors that point in that direction, such as the art of the time. Because of the trade which went on around the Mediterranean, several different cultures interacted with each other and the Minoans and Egyptians were no exceptions. A famous sarcophagus from around 1400 BC found at Hagia Triada showed this influence on one of the side panels. The burial was that of a noble or possibly even royalty, because his sarcophagus was made from stone and the illustrations were finely detailed. The goddess herself appears only on the narrow ends of the sarcophagus and taken as a whole the scenes prove conclusively the dominant role was played by women celebrants—even when the burial was that of a man. Whether they appear to be priestesses or court ladies or princesses, it is they who carry out the sacred acts of the libation, the sacrifice, and the offerings at the altar. The men are merely carriers of heavy objects, labourers, if you will.

As well as the sarcophagus found at Hagia Triada, a prime piece of evidence that supports the notion that Minoan women dominated the society were the Snake oddesses. An illustration of two such goddesses is shown in Logiadou Knossos: The Minoan Civilization, 68. As we can see, one is dressed in the flounced Minoan style and is holding out a snake in each hand and possibly with an owl on her hat. (In some photographs it actually looks rather like a pussy-cat.) Unfortunately this is something of a reconstruction by guesswork, since the left forearm and part of the hat were missing when it was discovered. So it would appear that we cannot be entirely certain that there was a snake in each hand—possibly the left contained the rest of the snake or something totally different, although the Minoan goddess was shown on other seals and statuettes holding a snake in each hand or wreathed tightly round her arms, and the symbol on the hat is a little nebulous as well. The other goddess is wearing a snake girdle, with snakes winding around her arms as we can see in the left hand illustration. Many scholars think that the principle female goddesses of Greek religion such as Hera, Artemis, and so on, are ultimately derived from the Minoan goddesses. If that is so, however, we have a potential link between Minoan and Amazon through the gods and goddesses mentioned in the dedications and on the Linear B tablets. There are dedications to gods and goddesses that are of considerable interest. They mention Zeus, Hera, Poseidon, Hermes, Athena, and Artemis. Even Dionysus crops up on two Linear B tablets at Pylos. We should remember that legend has it that Zeus as an infant, was hidden in a cave on Mount Ida in Crete and that Artemis, who figures as the virgin huntress and goddess of the moon, was his daughter. "She gives increase to all wild creatures and protects their young [ποτνια Θερον], and extends the same protection to flocks and herds and mankind: in this connexion, and as a lunar goddess, she is especially the goddess of women, their protector in childbirth [λοχια] and the giver of life and death" (Whibley, 1916, 391).

Like the Spartans and Amazons, Minoan women trained in all sorts of physical activities such as wrestling, boxing, and most dangerously, bull-jumping, also called taurokathapsia from the Greek ταυωκαθαψια. A fresco in colour dating from about 1500-1450 BC, shows a youth vaulting over the bull, with two white-skinned girls standing by as catchers. There is also a line drawing that shows how the gymnast may have performed the vault and the different stages of the "flight," as it were (Cottrell, 1961, plates 8 and 9). Some gemstone or clay seals also show young men attempting the same thing. These contests did not appear to expose the animal to harassment or to torture by being poked by sharp spears, nor did they culminate in the death of the bull, although it may have been sacrificed at some future time after the end of the celebrations. The contests were a test of both agility and courage and could well have served as a rite of passage. The most famous of these sports was the Thessalian ταυωκαθαψια in which men on horseback were engaged. Similar contest were also held in places such as Smyrna and Ankara during the classical period. It would seem that the Minoans could possibly have been the first "leisure" oriented society, since such a large part of their existence focussed on sport of one kind or another, including boxing, wrestling, and dancing.

Interestingly, a recent 2006 television programme "Tribe," concerned an Ethiopian tribal ritual of "cow-jumping," which is used today as a ritual rite of passage for the young men of the tribe. The origins of bull or cow-jumping may usefully be questioned. For example, did it originate in Crete and travel to Africa, or did it happen the other way around? Evans suggested that the Minoan civilization was somehow "kick-started" by an influx of Libyan refugees. Bearing in mind that the evidence of bull-fighting contests indicates that they have been found as far afield as China and the Indus Valley, their origin is wide open to investigation, as is the time when they originated. Perhaps there could be a link of some sort between Cretan and African cultures that would bear further investigation when we bear in mind that Libyans have been linked with Minoan Crete by Sir Arthur Evans.

In these Minoan frescoes and art in general, women are depicted much larger than the Minoan men, usually about twice the size, and are often shown with weapons, whereas men are not. The Minoan priesthood seems to have been composed mostly of women. Putting all these bits and pieces together, we have several of the elements that make up the Amazons. The double-headed axe carried by the Amazons has its counterpart in the labrys utilised by the Minoan priestesses and could indicate a possible link between the Amazon and Minoan cultures. Eventually, around the beginning of the Bronze Age patriarchal societies, possibly with male gods invaded and probably started to attempt the domination of the matriarchal system and their gods and goddesses. It is also more than likely that the females decided that they did not want to submit to a patriarchal culture and so started a rebellion against male domination and their system of religion. If we consider that the double-headed axe was a religious power object to the Minoans and that the Amazons often used it in battle, perhaps even as a symbol, a rallying point to be carried into battle, then the link between Minoans and Amazons could be seen to be a little less tenuous. It may be that the Amazons were simply a tribe or tribes of women who revolted against the enforcement of a patriarchy and the overthrow of their own goddesses, seeing it as part of the new order they despised.

Chapter 4

Modern Archaeology

Harking back to Herodotus and his description of the meeting of the Amazons and Scythians, we remember that after the shipwreck on the shore of Lake Maeotis, the two tribes finally came together and went off on their own. Herodotus tells us that they travelled east from the lake for three days and then north for three days, finally settling at that place. Lake Maeotis is the modern Sea of Azov, and if we look at a modern map, we can see that this area would have been in the Southern Ukraine, roughly where modern excavations are in progress. In fact, Professor Rolle has excavated at Bel'sk, roughly two hundred miles north of the lake. (Map 1). This is well inside the largest area shown that contains women warrior graves. Some of the graves excavated in Russia were incredibly rich in jewellery and gold artefacts as well as weapons, tools, food containers, horses, and slaves, which had all been buried with the personage concerned. Map 1 is of particular interest, because we can see not only some of the literary locations of the Amazons, but also the positions of the graves of women warriors, giving us a means of comparison between them. If we look at the map, we can see where the ancient writings place the various tribes of Amazons. The "Greek" Amazons, as it were, were based around the mouth of the Thermodon, in their city of Themiskyra on the southern coast of the Black Sea, which was one of the three major cities of the Northern Amazon Nation, in company with Chadesia and Lykastia. Other tribes of Amazons are shown on the western coastline of Turkey at Troy and Ephesus, and on the Mediterranean coast of Libya, where they are said to have lived on an island in Lake Tritonis. Diodorus Siculus says that "They lived on the island Hisperia, otherwise Tritonia, so called because it was situated in a fen called Tritonida from a river of that name which entered the ocean. The fen lay between Ethiopia and the Atlas [mountains]. It is generally assumed that by this the Hesperides, or Fortunate Isles [the modern Canaries], is intended, and this conjecture seems to be confirmed by the statement that Tritonia was a country subject to earthquakes and where, as it did in the Asiatic cradle of the Amazon race, flames belched forth from the ground. But the description given by our author appears rather to apply to an oasis in a marsh, or perhaps the Great Sahara, or an island detached from an alluvial delta." The current thinking is that Tritonis was the lake now called Chott Djerid, close to the Tunisian/ Algerian border, supposedly in the lands of the Libyan Amazons.

There have been several areas of investigation, one of which took place in the 1950s and 60s by Sergei Rudenko. He excavated five large kurgans (burial mounds) in the Altai Mountains in Kazakhstan, which he later identified as Pazyryk burials. The site consists of five large and nine small burial mounds dating from the fifth to the third century BC. The women whom were found there were dismissed by Rudenko as being simply the wives of the chiefs, and not women of power in their own right. Kimball found evidence of the existence of women warrior tribes on the Russian steppes, who could have conceivably corresponded to the classical Amazons.

Probably the most famous Pazyryk body to be found was that of the "Ice Princess," excavated by Natalia Polosmak in 1993.

As we can see from Map 1, there are two main areas of excavation, around Pokrovka and the larger area around Bel'sk north of the Sea of Azov. We need to look at the archaeology of both areas to see if there is anything which will support the Amazon theory, so let us look at the Pokrovka burials first. Sauromatians used to bury their dead here around 600 BC. It would also seem that after about 400 BC the mounds at Pokrovka were re-used by Sarmatians, who may have been related to the Sauromatians. However, Kimball also tells us of another major group of women whom had been entombed in the kurgans of Pokrovka. This group she called the priestesses and so we must be sure that nothing is dismissed out of hand. Assuming that the archaeologists are correct in their reasoning and their identification of the priestess graves, some three percent of the graves at Pokrovka were those of warrior-priestesses and of warrior-women, some fifteen percent. Because around seventy-five percent of the burials belonged to "women of the hearth," the indication is that the warriors were probably mainly in their teens and twenties, with the majority, the older women, in all likelihood looking after the home and children. The burials date from the Sauromatian Period, (sixth to fourth centuries BC), the Early Sarmatian Period (fourth to second centuries BC), the Middle Sarmatian Period (first century BC to first century AD) and to the Late Sarmatian Period (second to third centuries AD).

One of the graves excavated was that of a young warrior-priestess who was buried with her dagger, bronze arrowheads, and a quiver, and so we have an indication that warrior women did exist, at least in the Pokrovka area. This young female seems to have been quite a warrior, because she had these arrowheads, but also the dagger was made from iron, a scarce and valuable material at this time. This shows that her people had taken her training very seriously because of the rarity of the iron. It would not be given to everyone, only the best. She was interred with some fossilized sea-shells as well as the weaponry to possibly indicate her role as a priestess, but many other female warriors' graves contained none of these sea-shells at all, thus possibly indicating that a female warrior caste existed who had nothing to do with serving the religious life of the tribe and were simply fighters. Kimball's estimate was that this girl, for she was little more than that according to Leonid Yablonsky, a colleague of Kimball's, lived around 300 BC. (Kimball, 57).

Some of the women were buried with legs wide as though they were riding horses, maybe to emphasize their status as they moved on into the other world. Others had very bowed legs and fused vertebrae at the base of their spines, gained by a lifetime on horseback. Apart from their shells and armaments, the women's graves also contained items like beads, perfume bottles, and earrings. They may well have been bloodthirsty warriors, but at least they looked, and if the perfume bottles found in the graves are anything to go by, could well have smelled good while they were fighting. According to Kimball most of the warriors had been in their teens when they were killed, indicating an early start to their warrior training and thereby probably causing an early end to their lives. The numbers of arrowheads found in the graves would surely indicate that they preferred to use bows and arrows, probably whilst mounted, rather than engage in hand-to-hand combat, pretty much as the tales of the Amazons would have us believe. These tactics do make sense though, when we consider that a woman is typically of a slighter build than the male and probably would have somewhat lesser strength than the enemies they were fighting, but they would have been much more agile, which is pretty much what we would expect from horseback warriors. In some graves excavated by Rolle, it was found that women also wore a sort of armour, a heavy fighting belt covered with iron strips, in addition to arrows, lances, and the usual grave goods (perfume and cosmetic jars, bronze mirrors, and spinning accoutrements). Belts have been, and still are, important elements of dress, because they can delineate status, as well as the clan of the person wearing it. Traditional dress in modern times is often kaftans or heavy coats held together by an ornamented belt. Some of the buckles of silver or gold illustrate the Tree of Life, fantastic creatures, birds, and even people. This belt, of course, may equate to the zôstêr of the Amazons, a people that Rolle mentions more than once, even to the extent of telling us that many questions are left unanswered when trying to explain or interpret the Amazon graves, especially the question of whether or not the Amazons actually did exist. She also makes a rather sweeping statement that the graves in the steppes are generally accepted to be those of Amazons but unfortunately without telling us who accepts this. I would agree that graves of women warriors are to be found, but not those of Classical Amazons according to the legends. There are graves at Pokrovka of both male and female warriors that could maybe indicate that the classical Amazons described by Herodotus and others did not frequent this area, since they were supposed to have been a full matriarchy. It must be noted, however, that there is undeniable evidence that women warriors lived in the steppes area during the time of the Classical Amazons, but again, not identified as Amazon warriors. It is a distinct possibility that Herodotus knew of these women warriors, but had somehow confused them with older stories of a matriarchal people, giving rise to the Amazons of Classical Greece.

A considerable amount of Rolle's book is concerned with excavations in and around Bel'sk, north of Lake Maeotis, the modern Sea of Azov. B. N. Sramko, director of a team from the University of Khar'kov, is of the opinion that the modern Bel'sk is the city of Gelonus, which was said by Herodotus to be "far into the Scythian hinterland," and to have "wooden walls thirty furlongs long each way." The modern Bel'sk has ramparts, some of which were wooden walls seven metres high, some twenty point five miles in length and some buildings have been dated to the sixth century BC. It is in this area that most graves of women warriors have been found, as can be seen from the map.

The oldest known grave found dates from the fourth century BC and contained two skeletons. Nothing has as yet been proven to be Amazon. The female had her head pointed west as in other burials of note, but at her feet lay another, male, skeleton lying with his head towards the south as shown in Rolle, 1998, 88. In the grave were earrings and other items of jewellery, for example: bracelets on both of her wrists, iron knives, lance points, and arrowheads, mostly to the left of the body. But again, Rolle is conflating the terms "warrior women" and "Amazons" without providing anything in the way of proof, except that they were female warriors, which is not disputed and it seems as though there is some wishful thinking going on. It would appear that after the purported joining of the Scythians and Amazons, the Amazons per se did actually settle down with the men folk and became the founders of the Sauromatae, of whom Herodotus said, "Ever since then the women of the Sauromatae have kept to their old ways, riding to the hunt on horseback sometimes with, sometimes without, their menfolk, taking part in war and wearing the same sort of clothes as men" (Herodotus IV, 116). If you log on to the Internet and use the search argument "Amazon warriors DNA," it will find several web sites, one of which is http://www.thirteen.org/pressroom/pdf/sod/amazon/SOTDAmazonWarriorRelease.pdf. The information presented here concerns a "Mongolian Amazon Warrior Princess," which is probably jumping the gun a little. However, some of the bones discovered by Dr. Jeannine Davis-Kimball were disinterred, and their DNA was extracted by a German forensic anthropologist Joachim Burger. This DNA was compared with that of a living nine year old girl named Meiramgul and found to be identical. That means that we have definitive proof of a genetic link between this young twentieth century girl and the ancient warrior-priestesses discovered by Davis-Kimball.

So the early Amazons who lived and fought without men appear to have "mellowed" and moved on to the next phase of their existence, that of cohabitation with their male warrior equals. At least, this particular tribe did so, but others may have remained faithful to the old ways.

Chapter 5

Modern Amazons

Many other countries have tales of warrior women, although they were not specifically called Amazons, right down to the present day, and warrior women were well known in India and the Far East. A Greek ambassador, Megathenes, passed on information around 300 BC, in some fragments of his reports sent back to one of Alexander's lieutenants, Seleukotos Nikador, who tried with some success to continue in Alexander's footsteps after his death. He came up against a native chief or king whose personal bodyguard was composed of women armed with bows and arrows and who accompanied him when he went hunting. The women were mounted on horses and elephants or rode in chariots.

The Mahabharata, a sacred book of India, tells us of the times when Arjuna entered a land populated with women only. The custom here was for the women to keep the men for one month and then kill them, but the women who had not conceived during that month committed sutti, (suicide by immolation). The Mahabharata consists of a collection of religious and dynastic ballads dating back to around 1500 BC and from them we can see that tales of the Indian warrior women are very similar to those of the classical Amazons. For example, in approximately 300 BC an Indian emperor, Chandragupta Maurya, had a personal bodyguard composed of "giant"

Greek women. Boudicca (or Boadicea) became the ruler of the Iceni tribe of Norfolk after the death of her husband Prasutagas, a client king of the Romans. Because the Romans flogged her and raped her daughters, she took arms against them. The exact date of this is not known with certainty, but Tacitus placed it firmly in AD 61. Some modern historians agree with him, although others have a tendency to accept AD 60 as the correct date. Boudicca has been credited with the deaths of an estimated seventy thousand Romans and Romanized Celts before she was finally killed back in the first century AD. Tacitus tells us that she had a considerable number of women under arms, in fact a larger number than men in her army that revolted against the Romans, and so we can see that there has been a tradition of women warriors since before and after the fall of Troy.

The Times newspaper website carried a report from December 22, 2004, to the effect that the remains of two Amazon warriors serving with the Roman Army in Britain had been discovered in a cemetery near Brougham in Cumbria. The women were believed to have been from the Danube region and died around 220–300 AD. Because they were women and from the area of the Danube, they were immediately dubbed Amazons, but without any further proof to support that statement. The article would seem to be simply another example of the sensational press, taking the basic verifiable facts and sensationalising them as only journalists can. However, Kimball has a theory that a Roman detachment of some five thousand Sarmatian tribesmen were sent to the north of England to guard Hadrian's Wall. A web site that one could look at is www.europabarbarorum.com/factions_sauromatae_history.html. If true, they would have been accompanied by their wives and children, thus accounting for the bodies of the women who were found (Kimball, 2002, 32). Even today, President Gadaffi of Libya has a personal guard of female soldiers. In a statement issued on March 8, 2006, JANA said, "Within the framework of upgrading the capabilities of armed people associates and to break the monopoly of military knowledge and building strike force in compliance with the recommendations of the Basic People's Congresses and in line with the chart of the declaration of People's Authority that defending the homeland is the responsibility of every male and female citizen a ceremony was held Tuesday morning marking the graduation of new batch of general military training of female associates at the people's defence centres in different Shabias of Libya." New Amazons are popping up on a regular basis, as we can see from this press release and are unlikely to just go away.

Again, there are many more examples of less ancient warrior women like Jeanne d'Arc and not least more modern characters such as Xena, Warrior Princess. If we consider Xena and her sidekick Gabrielle, I think it fairly obvious that their characters are based on old Amazon stories, as are the television tales of Hercules and his feuding with Hera and other gods and goddesses, in between fights with warrior women. If we add male impersonators to the equation, Great Britain has had its fair share of them. Some, like Miss Vesta Tilley, were popular stars of the music hall era, but others did actually bear arms. Vesta Tilley strutted across the London stage during the Great War, dressed in military uniform and singing martial songs which hopefully kept up people's spirits, but she was never a warrior. On the opposite side of the coin we find Flora Sandes. She became a soldier of the Serbian Army during the Great War and the following years until her demobilisation in 1922. Sandes was wounded both in Tunisia and in Monastir, and her reputation helped her fund-raising activities to gain British aid for Serbia and funds to relieve suffering there. Her activities and record indicate that she was the very epitome of a modern Amazon Warrior. In fact, I think she could have held her head up with pride in the company of the Ancient Amazon warriors had they existed (Wheelwright, 1989). More than that, she could hold up her head in any company. There are many other modern examples that we could use, but these two suffice to illustrate both types—the male impersonator and the true female warrior.

There are several websites, mainly American I should add, that deal with the question of Amazons and their relevance to the modern world, which we will look at in due course. The legends of the Amazons seem to have taken hold of our imaginations, and many women worldwide appear to be attempting to carry on those legends regardless of whether or not the original legends were based in fact, as we can see from television series like Xena and Hercules.

The Classical Amazons governed and sustained their own people and communities, and although the modern Amazons sustain and govern their own to a degree, the modern Amazon websites appear to have more to do with female bodybuilders for the most part, rather than with the true Amazon nature. There are many sites on the Internet that are dedicated to "art" poses and photographs, but substantially fewer teach the ethic of wanting to be or being an Amazon. Using a search argument of "modern amazons" on Google or on Yahoo will identify different sites in each category. For example, the website located at www.absolutearts.com will explain that: "Picturing the Modern Amazon is a collaboration between women bodybuilders, athletes, artists, scholars, feminists, and historians." Unfortunately, there does not appear to be much input either from scholars or historians when we investigate a site that will provide images of the bodybuilders mentioned, to be found at the web site address: http://www.femalemuscle.com/contests/amazons.html. I think that you can see from this that a great emphasis is put upon female bodily perfection—the paragon of the modern superficial Amazons. However, perhaps that is not the whole story. According to Kleinbaum, 1983, 224, the Amazon image was composed of political power, military skill, their autonomy, and hence the dignity of their way of life.

Film and cartoon characters have been based on stories with an Amazon background, like Katharine Hepburn, who made her Broadway debut as an Amazon princess back in 1941. Wonder Woman is another example. This character first turned up in 1940s and the more modern TV short film versions of the seventies starred Linda Carter in the title role. She played an Amazon princess, ostensibly the daughter of Queen Hippolyte, and was a super heroine cast in the mould of Superman. Her alter ego, Diana, a mild mannered secretary was the direct equivalent of Superman's Clark Kent, another mild mannered reporter. Another famous character was that of Buck Rogers, who found himself stranded on Zantia, a planet of super warrior women. So in modern times, the Amazon is taken far from seriously in most cases, being used primarily for entertainment and self aggrandisement purposes.

The Amazons have also been adopted by another type of woman, those who have lesbian leanings and who appear to be genuine man haters who wish to live their lives as did the Amazons of classical times. They are apparently in pursuit of some sort of self determination and wear a "labrys" (double headed axe of the classical Amazons) as a symbol of belonging. Some also wear a single earring, such as appears in illustrations on the classical Greek vases. In fact, the single earring in the illustration on the vase is quite a sure identification that we are looking at an Amazon warrior. Lesbians adopted the labrys as a symbol of power and independence. The labrys is also known as a πελεκυς in Greek and as a bipennis to the Romans. In modern days other symbols have, to an extent, supplanted the traditional, and many different countries have their own form. The modern world does not, however, allow such departure from law and order in the main, and so we have some small groups of fanatics who subvert the old ways and bend them to their own use—or misuse, as the case may be. Looking a little further, however, we will find one of several important websites, the address of which is: www.modernamazons.org.uk.

Some others are listed in the bibliography, for example IN Ref 26 and 27. The story changes a little here, when we discover that the Amazons are being used as an exhibition, a charity, and also to bring important information to the attention of women worldwide. This information has to do with breast cancer and stories with a positive outcome that have an uplifting effect on the women who read them, at the same time the website throws out a lifeline for those who may be worried about the disease. A phone number and email address are provided for those who wish to contact any of the support sites on the list provided. And so we can see that all is not simply vanity, lesbianism, self determination, or what have you, but it can be, and in this case, it is about fighting a deadly enemy. I suspect that the classical Amazons would have approved.

Chapter 6

Conclusion

Down through the years, memories and rumours of the Classical Amazons have been persistently located in the Pontus region along the south coast of the Black Sea and in the Caucasus range of mountains. After all of the defeats the Amazons suffered, some are said to have taken refuge in the higher mountains and carried on with their own way of life as far as possible. The almost inaccessible fortress of Karpu Kale, perched on a mountain top as it is, is associated with the Amazons after they had more or less withdrawn from patriarchal cultures that were trying to dominate their way of life. There were many reports of fighting women in these regions and when Mithridates V, King of Pontus, although not at the time of the Classical Amazons, fought against the Romans in around 100 BC, he had women warriors in his army. After the fighting was over Appianus, in his account of the war says, "There were found among the prisoners and hostages several women whose wounds were as great and as dangerous as those of the men. These women were said to be Amazons." In 1796 Jacob Reineggs said that before his forefathers had come to the Black Sea, the land was in the possession of women who "Were without men, but, full of warlike spirit associated themselves with any woman who cared to share their wanderings and to join their heroic guild" (Rothery, 1910, Ch.5).

The fighting ability of the warrior in ancient societies was often used to determine social status within the tribe. The better the fighter, the more plunder and riches obtained and the more he or she was looked up to. Obviously then, the richer the warrior the more the influence and the higher he or she climbed in the tribal position. The fighting style of the Greek and Roman warrior favoured men because of the requirement for upper body strength, but the fighting style that was attributed to the Amazons favoured the women much more. Horseback archers, lithe and agile, could compete very favourably with the men because of the speed of attack and retreat and the fact that hand-to-hand combat was not usually a requirement of their battles. By their speedy attack and retreat they could decimate the armies they were fighting against. Their style made them very effective killers, equal to the men, and gave them a much higher status than they would otherwise have had if they had simply been wives and mothers. Horses and bows and arrows in conjunction with their warlike spirit empowered these women to be a serious threat to the soldiers on the battlefield. During the eighth and seventh centuries BC, Cimmerians raided the area along the south coast of the Black Sea and Wilde says it is possible that their women were warriors who started the tradition of Amazons in this area, but it is very much supposition on her part. Likewise, Reinache was another who thought that the Cimmerians served as models for the Amazon warriors. Another idea of Amazon female power can possibly be traced back to the Hittites as well. The Hittites were a world power at the time of the Trojan War, but their empire broke up shortly thereafter and became insignificant by the time of Classical Greece. It has been postulated that the women warriors were simply beardless

Hittite warriors, who in the heat of battle were mistaken for women. The Hittites also wore their hair long in a similar fashion to Greek women, so perhaps this was a factor of their identification as well. However, in contrast, we are told that the "Anatolian Amazons whom the Greeks originally encountered are portrayed more accurately in their battle gear by the Hittites. In great murals . . . the Hittites showed the Amazons in feather crested or cone-shaped helmets" (IN Ref 16, 10). Surely this is an indication that Hittites and Amazons were not one and the same people. Blok tells us that, after an investigation into the cults, with whom the Amazons were closely related, Florence Mary Bennett rejected the idea of clean-shaven Hittite men being mistaken for women.

This would appear to somewhat support Rostovzeff's explanation of the Amazons, which was that rather than identifying them as Cimmerians or clean-shaven Hittites, simply connect matriarchal societies wherever there was a cult of the Mother Goddess. This is a debatable point, since the Mother Goddess appears in many different cultures that were not necessarily matriarchal. Essentially therefore, what Rostovzeff appears to be saying is that each tribe of Amazons, whether or not they actually founded them, was related to and grew up around these various cults (Rostovzeff, 1922). As I said, the Mother Goddess was a feature of many cultures, and it is possible that the Greek goddesses were developed from an earlier culture, maybe from a process of acculturation, linked with the feminine Minoans and the masculine Mycenaeans. This Mother Goddess aspect could certainly explain the number of different tribes of Amazons that were ascribed to Europe and the Middle East, but it would tend to fall down somewhat when we consider the

Far Eastern countries that also had traditions of warrior women, such as the armed guards in service with the various eastern potentates. In these particular cases, the women were part and parcel of a patriarchal system; they served the men, did not live alone, and as such could not be called true Amazons, but were simply female warriors. Warrior women have been recorded in many different cultures throughout the world, and while most tend to be located in Europe and Africa, we do have some accounts of them in the Middle East, the Far East, South America, and Great Britain, as already mentioned. Written records dating from 1500 BC, according to Elphinstone, have been collected by the Brahmin priests of India and put together to form an Indian sacred book, the Mahabharata, which contains stories of warrior women and so our potential Amazon time frame has been extended a little more (IN Ref 29).

There have been several geographical areas recorded in which there were women only, living apart from men. For example, Palladius, Bishop of Hellenopolis in his De Gentibus Indiae, wrote that Brahmin men in the valley of the Ganges lived on one side of the river and the women on the other. The men apparently visited them for forty days every June, July, and August, but when a child was born the man never returned. This, one could think, would seem to be a rather garbled account of Amazon life put together from various tales of the riverbank. However, all or most of the tales of men and women living apart for most of the year may well be true if we stop to think about the practicalities of life. I think it entirely possible that the menfolk could have spent time away preparing ground for growing their food supplies and tending crops, only going home for brief periods of time when the seasons would allow. During the

absences of the men, the women would need to be prepared to defend their homes and children if necessary
and with the absence of their men would undoubtedly
tend to become quite self-sufficient and independent.
Given these conditions it is quite possible for travellers
who did not know or understand the areas they were
passing through to add two and two and achieve the
impossible.

Another account, perhaps slightly more credible,
comes to us from the patriarch Bermudes, who refers to
an island in the South China Seas that is "inhabited by
Amazons, who in the usual way, only received men at
stated seasons, keeping the girls born to them and send-
ing the boys to their fathers" (IN Ref 29). There is nothing mentioned about when the boys were sent or taken
away. Possibly they were retained until they achieved a
minimum age that would enable them to be looked after
by the older boys who were already with the men. Why
should this not be the case? The men would certainly
benefit from the potential extra labourers and would be
glad of any extra help they could get in order to eke out
a living and provide the necessary sustenance for themselves and their families. Other locations are mentioned
by various scholars as places of women only, but the
evidence for Amazon matriarchies is slim. Since an
investigation of these claims would in all probability
provide enough material for a book on this one subject,
an investigation into these areas is probably too much
for a basic introduction to the Amazons.

Some of the graves excavated at Pokrovska and
Bel'sk were those of priestesses, as well as warrior
priestesses, indicating worship of a Mother Goddess,
possibly Artemis as previously mentioned, since they
have been interpreted as having a connection with the

cult of Artemis in Ephesus. Artemis and Cybele were both moon goddesses, and because the moon is also associated with women, it would appear quite natural for the Amazons to worship one or both of them. The religious health of the community could have been looked after by the ordinary priestesses in conjunction with the warrior priestesses, who might also have had some sort of extra, special, responsibilities when going into battle or in defence of their people. Not all graves contained accoutrements such as the fossilized seashells, which possibly indicated their calling, but having said this, we should remember that including fossilized seashells amongst their burial possessions may not necessarily indicate the fact that they were priestesses. Seashells could mean something totally different, and no positive evidence has been presented as to their meaning, except that they are associated with unbroken mirrors, which were probably assumed to be useful for scrying in the next life, along with miniature stone or clay altars, and so the fossilized sea shells are linked to the office of priestess by association only. It is possible, though, that they were in fact warrior priestesses who looked after the secular life of the tribe and left the others to minister to the religious life.

However, if we look closely at the illustration of the reconstruction of the shrine of the Minoan Snake Goddess by Sir Arthur Evans, we can see that he has utilised a considerable number of seashells (Ref 31 for image). There is no description of the shrine other than the photograph to explain the items shown, but there appears to be a mixture of oyster, clam, and cowry shells. and so perhaps Evans has recognised their appropriateness for his reconstruction. Taking this idea a little further, could this indicate a link from Minoan Crete to the excavations at Pokrovska, or indeed Russia in general? Could this, in fact, be confirmation that the seashells were indeed a sign of a priestess, a warrior, or otherwise? Unfortunately, there is no evidence to say that these graves were those of the classical Amazons, although some of the grave goods found bear a resemblance to items attributed to the Amazons. As an example, the metalled belts found in some graves could be seen to be the equivalent of the legendary zôstêr of the Amazons. We are also told that the finds included iron daggers or knives, which bears out the assertion of Lysias during his Funeral Oration (Lamb, 1930, 2.4). Graves of other warrior priestesses have also been recorded at Filippovka, Issyk, Prokorovka, Tillya Tepe, and in the Tien Shan Mountains.

The nomads who performed the burial rites had an unshakeable belief in the after world, which is why the graves contained items other than just bodies. Some provisions were included, as were their tools and accoutrement that they had gathered together during their earthly lives so that they would be comfortably off in the next world. I rather suspect that having reached the "top" in this life they would not be at all anxious to start again at the bottom in the next world, and so they were given a helping hand, as it were, to make an auspicious start to their next life. The beliefs of these people are extremely useful to us, because the artefacts and ethnographic information we uncover can provide much information and allow us to see a little way into their culture, lives, and deaths. Some graves included the remains of valuable horses in huge quantities. Back in 1898 at an excavation in Aul Ul' in the Caucasus three hundred and sixty horse skeletons were found in one tomb, thus showing the wealth of the chieftain or king who was buried there. Another excavation of a kurgan at Arïan lasted from 1971 until 1974, such was the immense size of it. There were seventy interlocking chambers in a circular foundation, but unfortunately the mound had been plundered by grave robbers. However, what was found were the bodies of a king and queen resting on about fifteen to twenty horsetails and accompanied by the skeletons of over a hundred and fifty horses (Rolle, 1989, 38–46).

Some of the trappings have been reconstructed from scraps found in the burial mounds, and it can be seen that they were extremely richly and beautifully decorated (Rolle, 1989, Ch.5 shows how the trappings were reconstructed). This rich decoration may well be because of the nomadic existence of the tribes and the fact of them having nowhere to display their wealth, except if they wear it or carry it with them and use their everyday lives to put on a show, as it were. This again shows the importance of horses to the nomads, that they should decorate them so richly and have such vast herds that so many could be spared to accompany the royal couple into the afterlife. This would argue for the fact that all of the tribe, women and children included could, and did ride horses. So as a logical extension of that I can see no reason why the womenfolk would not have been expected to help out the men with whatever required doing, be it looking after the herds or protecting them from raiders.

Considering all of the archaeological evidence so far unearthed, I think it safe to say that tribes of warrior women did actually exist in the ancient world, albeit in conjunction with male warriors. The excavations at Pokrovka and Bel'sk provide the necessary proof of this. However, there is no indication that they were matriarchies, since we have evidence that the burial sites contained both male and female warriors. This, of course, does not prove that this was not a matriarchy, especially when we remember the warrior priestesses and the old legends that the women maimed the men in some fashion, as a measure of self-protection. They could then have continued to live in proximity with each other, using the men as slaves.

In light of all of the evidence the inescapable conclusion is that while there were undoubtedly races of women warriors, there is no proof that they were the Amazon warriors of antiquity. At least, not the Amazons as described by Herodotus and the others. What is probably more likely is that the young girls were trained almost from birth to take their place as fully fledged warriors alongside the menfolk in war and peace. This is what happens today in Kazakhstan, where boys and girls between the ages of six and nine traditionally race horses over a distance of between fifteen and twenty-two miles, after having already ridden that distance just to reach the starting point. Socrates could almost have been talking about the warrior women in general when he said, "Men and women will serve together, and take the children to war with them when they are old enough, to let them see, as they do in other trades, the job they will have to do when they grow up." The Ancient Greeks perhaps knew of one or more of these cultures and, misread the signs, attributing them to a race of women warriors in which women were the dominant force. So far, scholars and archaeologists have no empirical or direct proof for or against a matriarchal race of Amazons, and I suspect that this is unlikely to change very much in the near future.

All in all then, in accepting the grave goods and accoutrement found in the female burials there is indisputable evidence for the existence of warrior women, who may or may not be descendants of the Sarmatians and Sauromatians, but unlike the tales of the Ancient Amazons they lived, rode, and fought with their menfolk. This is very similar to the situation in modern Kazakhstan, where the children are taught to ride from about one year old and upwards. They are also taught to use a bow and arrow, but combat has long since gone by the wayside. They could, in fact, be the modern version of the Sauromatian descendants of the Classical Amazons as we know from the mitochondrial DNA results.

So therefore, I should think that the existence of the Classical Amazon Warriors still awaits incontrovertible proof, but equally, tales of the Amazons will continue to captivate our imagination for some time to come.

Bibliography

Ancient Sources

Adams. F. (trans) undated. Hippocrates: On Airs, Waters and Places, Kessinger.

Boardman, J. 1967. Pre-Classical; From Crete to Archaic Greece, Harmondsworth, Penguin Books.

Boardman, J. 1974. Athenian Black Figure Vases, London, Thames and Hudson.

Boardman, J. 1975. Athenian Red Figure Vases: The Archaic Period, London, Thames and Hudson.

Boardman, J. 1978. Greek Sculpture, the Archaic Period, London, Thames and Hudson.

Boardman, J. 1989. Greek Art (Revised edition), London, Thames and Hudson Buschor, E. 1962 Bilderwelt Griechisher Tôpfer Munich, Piper & Co.

de Selincourt, A. (trans) 1996. Herodotus: The Histories Harmondsworth, Penguin Books.

Fagles, R. (trans) 1977. Aeschylus, The Oresteia, Harmondsworth, Penguin Books.

Fagles, R. (trans) 1990. The Iliad: Homer, USA, Penguin Books.

Fagles, R. (trans) 1997. The Odyssey: Homer, USA, Penguin Books.

Graves, R. (trans) 1992. The Greek Myths, Complete Edition, Harmondsworth, Penguin Books.

Green, D. and Lattimore, P. 1968 (eds). Greek Tragedies, Vol.1, London, Chicago University of Chicago Press.

Hard, R. 1997. Apollodorus: The Library, Oxford, OUP.

Lamb, W.R.M. 1930. Lysias, Cambridge, Mass. Harvard University Press.

Lee, H.D.P. (trans) 1956. Plato: The Republic, Harmondsworth, Penguin Books.

Levi, P. (trans) 1971. Pausanias: Guide to Greece, Harmondsworth, Penguin Books.

Morwood, J. (trans). 1998. Euripides: Medea and other Plays. Oxford, Oxford University Press.

Petrakos, B. 1998. National Museum; Sculpture-Bronzes-Vases, Athens, Clio.

Pottier, E. undated. Douris et les Peintres de Vases Grecs Paris, Libraire Renouard.

Rasmussen, T. & Spivey, N. 1997 (eds). Looking at Greek Vases, Cambridge, University Press.

Rawson, E. 1973. Life in Ancient Greece, London, Longman Group.

Scott-Kilvert, I. (trans) 1960. The Rise and Fall of Athens: Nine Greek Lives by Plutarch, Harmondsworth, Penguin Books.

Schwab, G. 1947. Gods & Heroes, London, Routledge.

Smith, R.R.R. 1995. Hellenistic Sculpture, London, Thames & Hudson.

Sommerstein, A. 1973. Aristophanes: Lysistrata/The Acharnians/The Clouds, Harmondsworth, Penguin Books.

Taylor, J. 1829. A Summary of Herodotus London, John Taylor.

Warner, R. (trans) 1972. Thucydides: History of the Peloponnesian War, Harmondsworth, Penguin Books.

Modern Sources

Alsop, J. 1964. From the Silent Earth, London, Secker & Warburg.

Andrews, A. 1967. Greek Society, Harmondsworth, Penguin Books.

Aptheker, B. 1989. Tapestries of Life, Amherst, University of Massachusetts Press.

Bennett, F.M. 1912. Religious Cults Associated with the Amazons, New York, Columbia University Press.

Blok, J. H. 1995. The Early Amazons: Modern and Ancient Perspectives on a Persistent Myth. Leyden, Brill.

Blundell, S. 1995. Women in Ancient Greece, London, British Museum Press.

Boardman, J. J Griffin & O. Murray. 2001. Oxford History of Greece and the Hellenistic World, Oxford, OUP.

Boardman, J., J. Griffin & O. Murray. 1990. Oxford History of the Classical World Oxford, OUP.

Brooke, I. 2003. Costume in Ancient Greek Drama, New York, Dover Pubs.

Browning, R. (ed) 1985. The Greek World, London, Guild Publishing.

Burkert, W. 1985. Greek Religion, Oxford, Blackwell Publishers.

Burckhardt, J. 1998. The Greeks & Greek Civilisation, Harper Collins.

Cartledge, P. 1993. The Greeks, Oxford, Oxford University Press.

Cartledge, P. 2002. The Spartans, London, Channel 4 Books.

Conacher, D. J. 1989. Aeschylus' Oresteia—A Literary Commentary, Toronto, University of Toronto Press.

Cook, R. M. 1972. Greek Art; Development, Character and Influence, Harmondsworth, Penguin Books.

Cottrell, L. 1961. The Bull of Minos, London, Evans Brothers.

Cottrell, L. 1963. The Lion Gate, London, Evans Brothers.

CD-ROM. 2003. Encyclopaedia Britannica.

Davies, J. K. 1993. Democracy and Classical Greece, London, Fontana Press.

Davis-Kimball, J. 2002. Warrior Women, New York, Warner Books Inc.

Ferguson, J. & K. Chisholm. 1978. Political and Social Life in the Great Age of Athens, Open University set book.

Fiada, A. 2000. Xenophobe's Guide to the Greeks, London, Oval Books.

Gantz, T. 1993. Early Greek Myth—A Guide to Literary and Artistic, Baltimore and London, Johns Hopkins University Press.

Gardner, P. 1905. A Grammar of Greek Art, London, Macmillan Co.

Goldhill, S. 1986. Reading Greek Tragedy, Cambridge, Cambridge University Press.

Graves, R. 1960. The Greek Myths, Harmondsworth, Penguin Books.

Grant, M. 1995. The Ancient Historians, London, Duckworth & Co.

Grant, M. 1997. The Rise of the Greeks, London, Orion Books Ltd.

Guerber, H. A. 1912. The Myths of Greece and Rome London, Harrap & Co.

Guhl, E. & W. Koner. 1994. The Greeks; Their Life and Customs, London, Studio Editions.

Gulick, C. B. 1903. The Life of the Ancient Greeks, New York & London, Appleton.

Hammond, N.G.L. 1959. A History of Greece, Oxford, OUP.

Hardy, D. (trans) undated. Knossos, the Minoan Civilisation, Athens, Mathioulakis & Co.

Harris, N. 2000. History of Ancient Greece, London, Hamlyn.

Harvey, P. 1962. Oxford Companion to Classical Literature, London, Oxford University Press.

Hawkes, J. 1972. Dawn of the Gods, London, Sphere Books.

Higgins, R. 2005. Minoan & Mycenaean Art, Thames and Hudson, London.

Hornblower, S. 1991. The Greek World. 479–323 BC, London, Routledge.

Hornblower, S. & A. Spawforth. 1998. Oxford Companion to Classical Civilisation, Oxford, Oxford University Press.

Halperin, D., J. J. Winkler, F. I. Zeitlin, (eds). 1990. Before Sexuality, Princeton, N. J., Princeton University Press.

Lefkowitz, M. 1986. Women in Greek Myth, London, Duckworth.

Lefkowitz, M. & M. Fant. 1977. Women in Greece and Rome, Toronto, Samuel-Stevens.

Lempriere, J. 1911. A Classical Dictionary, London, Routledge.

Levi, P. 1989. Atlas of the Greek World, Oxford, Equinox Ltd.

Liddell, H. G. & R. Scott. 1866. A Greek-English Lexicon, Oxford, OUP.

Livingstone, R. W. 1915. The Greek Genius, Oxford, Clarendon Press.

Mendelsohn, D. 2005. Gender and the City in Euripides' Political Plays Oxford, OUP.

Mills, S. 1997. Theseus, Tragedy & the Athenian Empire, Oxford, Clarendon Press.

Mongait, A. L. 1961. Archaeology in the USSR, Harmondsworth, Penguin Books Murnaghan, S. 2000, Tantalus Symposium. University of Pennsylvania.

Murray, O. 1993. Early Greece, London, Fontana Press.

Norwood, G. 1964. Greek Comedy, London, Methuen & Co. Ltd.

Oswalt. 1965. Collins Concise Encyclopaedia of Greek and Roman Mythology, London, Larousse.

Penguin. 1982. Map of the World, Michael Graham Pubs.

Phoca, I. 1992. Greek Pottery, Athens, Kedros.

Pinsent. 1969. Greek Mythology, London, Hamlyn.

Pomeroy, S. 1975. Goddesses, Whores, Wives and Slaves, London, Pimlico.

Pfuhl, E. 1955. Masterpieces of Greek Drawing & Painting, London, Chatto & Windus.

Richter, G. 1959. A Handbook of Greek Art, London, Phaidon.

Rolle, Prof. R. 1998. The World of the Scythians, Berkeley & Los Angeles, University of California Press.

Rose, H. J. 1946. Ancient Greek Religion, London, Hutchinson.

Rostovzeff, M. I. 1922. Iranians and Greeks in South Russia, Oxford, OUP.

Rothery, G. C. 1910. The Amazons, London, Griffiths.

Schuchhardt, W-H. 1990. Greek Art, London, Herbert Press.

Schwab, G. 1947. Gods and Heroes, London, Routledge.

Sealey, R. 1976. A History of the Greek City States, Berkeley, University of California Press.

Smith, W. 1870. A Smaller History of Greece, London, John Murray.

Smith, Sir W. 1895. A History of Greece, London, John Murray.

Snodgrass, M. A. 1988. Greek Classics, Nebraska, Cliffs Notes Inc.

Sommerstein, A. 2002. Greek Drama and Dramatics, London & New York, Routledge.

Spivey, N. 1997. Greek Art, London, Phaidon Press.

Stark, F. 1954. Ionia; A Quest, London, John Murray.

Stobart, J. C. 1980. The Glory that was Greece, London, BCA.

Taplin, O. 1978. Greek Tragedy in Action, Los Angeles, University of California Press.

Taylor, J. 1829. A Summary of Herodotus, London, John Taylor.

Tyrrell, W. B. 1984. Amazons: A Study in Athenian Mythmaking, Baltimore and London, Johns Hopkins University Press.

Vellacott, P. 1959. The Oresteian Trilogy, Harmondsworth, Penguin Books.

Vellacott, P. 1963. Euripides: Medea and Other Plays, Harmondsworth, Penguin Books.

Vernant, J-P. 1990. Myth and Society in Ancient Greece, New York, Zone Books.

Vivier, F. 2004. Greek Mythology Rochester,Kent. Grange Books PLC.

Warner, R. 1979. The Stories of the Greeks, St. Albans, Granada.

Webster-Wilde, L. 1999. On The Trail of the Women Warriors, London, Constable and Co.

Wettan-Kleinbaum, A. 1983. The War Against the Amazons New York, McGraw-Hill.

Whibley, L. 1916. A Companion to Greek Studies, Cambridge, University Press.

Wheelwright, J. 1989. Amazons and Military Maids, London, Pandora Press.

Wiles, D. 2000. Greek Theatre Performance, Cambridge, University Press.

Williams, H. S. 1907. The Historians History of the World, Vol. 111, London, The Times.

Winkler, J. J. 1990. The Constraints of Desire, London, Routledge.

Woodford, S. 1986. An Introduction to Greek Art, London, Duckworth & Co.

Willetts, R. F. 1977. Civilization of Ancient Crete, The, London, Batsford Ltd.

A. P. Bristol

Internet Sources

Internet sources can be hard to find at times. If any of these addresses return a 404 error, you will know they have been moved, and you will need to search for them. Go to the top level address and try from there.

www.stoa.org/diotima

www.pygmalion project.tripod.com/amazons.html

www.tx.essortment.com/amazonswarrior_ryci.htm

www.womanwarrior.co.uk

www.sacred-texts.com/stbib.htm

www.jstor.org

www.csen.org

www.mnsu.edu

www.myrine/at/amazons/maps_e.html

www.en.wikipedia.org/wiki/amazons

www.en.wikipedia.org/wkik/scythians

www.myrine/at/amazons/libya.html

www.moonspeaker.ca/Amazons/culture.html

www.depts.washington.edu/silkroad/museums/shm/
    shmpazyryk.html

www.en.wikipedia.org/wiki/amazons

www.lisasmedman.topcities.com/amazon02.pdf

www.budplant.com

www.xenite.org

www.google.co.uk

www.indopedia.org/amazons.html

www.modernamazons.org.uk

www.femalemuscle.com/contests/amazons.html

www.perseus.tufts.edu/cgi-bin/image?lookup=1991.07.1039

www.sacred-texts.com/wmn/ama/ama05.htm

www.archaeology.org/9701/abstracts/sarmatians.html

www.whoosh.org/issue12/ruffel3.html#listing

www.azer.com/aiweb/categories/magazine/
ai131_folder/131_articles

www.ancienthistory.about.com/od/homeschoolers/
a/majorevents_p.htm

www.en.wikipedia.org/wiki/minoan_civilization

www.net4you.net/user/poellauerg/amazons

http://witcombe.sbc.edu/snakegoddess/snakecharmers.html

www.azer.com/aiweb/categories/magazine/ai131_folder/
131_articles/131_amazons.html

www.fjkluth.com/amaz2.html

Index

Lightning Source UK Ltd.
Milton Keynes UK
UKHW021815040919
349131UK00001B/11/P